this author was with us
on Saipan, June 44, &
Iwo Jima, Feb. 45.

I am sure he was the
correspondant that took the
picture & wrote the right up
of me in Maui Hawaii
after the battle of Iwo.

The picture is in my
photo album.

Dennis Charlton

P9-CFL-662

From the Battlefield

Dan Levin

NAVAL INSTITUTE PRESS
Annapolis, Maryland

Dispatches of a

From the Battlefield

World War II Marine

© 1995 by Dan Levin

All rights reserved. No part of this book may be reproduced without written permission from the publisher.

Library of Congress Cataloging-in-Publication Data

Levin, Dan.
   From the battlefield : dispatches of a World War II marine / Dan Levin.
         p.   cm.
   ISBN 1-55750-515-2
   1. Levin, Dan.   2. World War, 1939–1945—Campaigns—Pacific Area.
3. World War, 1939–1945—Personal narratives, American.   4. War
correspondents—United States—Biography.   5. United States.   Marine
Corps—Biography.   I. Title.
D767.9.L48L48   1994
940.54′26—dc20   94-19370
                                                                                          CIP

Printed in the United States of America on acid-free paper ⊗

9 8 7 6 5 4 3 2   First printing

Passages have been adapted from Dan Levin's novels *Mask of Glory* and *The Dream in the Flesh*. Several of the poems were published in *Scimitar and Song* magazine. The article about the airfield on Tinian, from which the atomic bombers took off, first appeared in the *New York Times*.

The speech over the graves on Iwo Jima, since then widely reprinted, was that of Roland B. Gittelsohn, U.S. Navy chaplain with the Marines. He is now Rabbi Emeritus of Temple Israel in Boston.

Contents

1. The Father of All Things   **1**

2. Island of the Dead   **10**

3. We and They   **24**

4. Ghost Marines   **39**

5. Destination Iwo   **49**

6. Days of Wrath   **63**

7. Chronicle of Blood   **84**

8. The Long Road Back   **110**

9. The War God's Legacy   **122**

From the Battlefield

1–The Father of All Things

There are always reasons why someone becomes a Marine.

I became a Marine in World War II.

As a young radical of the thirties, I had been sustained by faith in communism until it broke under the blows of truth. In 1940 I was marooned in a land of disenchantment, with the country still mired in the Great Depression and all doors to my chosen career in journalism closed.

And with the approach of war, the WPA (Works Progress Administration)—President Roosevelt's safety net for the many millions of unemployed like me—was being phased out. There seemed to be no road ahead.

Nothing could come of me, I was sure, unless a great and overriding fate intervened.

1

For some winter weeks, I went out at midnight into cold Cleveland streets to wait for a 1 A.M. streetcar that took me to a high school. I was there until 5 A.M., learning to run a lathe. This was Retraining.

It would mean work, maybe, in a defense plant. I had gone through too much by then and had little heart for this, though I tried to be eager. I took a half-dozen civil service exams, got top grades in all of them—and heard no more.

Until one day a telegram arrived. I tore it open with fumbling hands. I could be a prison guard in a federal jail; reply at once.

I had not aimed for this either. I could not imagine replying.

In a last gasp, I went to live with relatives in Washington, carrying my civil service scores. These made no difference— I had no connections, knew no congressmen.

Suddenly Pearl Harbor came.

In the confusion of Washington in the next weeks, and with a stroke of luck in one of sixty interviews—there was a job!

Everything changed. I could show my skills, do interesting work. And in that frenetic wartime town, once you were in you could move—as I did—from an old-line department to a war agency, at better pay.

War, the ancient Greek philosopher Heracleitus said, is the Father of all things, Maker and Savior. How could I not be grateful to the war that had saved me and would make me. A romantic idealist, I now believed in this war, embracing it as a war against Nazism and fascism, a righteous war unlike any other. I would feel free to paint it in glorious colors, with all its awfulness. I had already been writing fervid poems that looked forward to falling

one among myriads, anonymous,
shielding the rose of freedom with my heart.

That is not to say an inner conflict did not go on. I also wrote, suddenly, hardly knowing what I was scribbling—

Tear down your banners and gag the drums!
The spirits still cry with grief.
You can right every wrong but never return
Blood to the throat, green to the leaf.

This insight would hound me, much later.

But for now, war would render great service to me as it did to many. In my green uniform I could leave behind my disappointments over career, quandaries over marriage, and struggles over identity. War could even give me my theme, for I needed a theme in order to become a writer. I seized the chance as if I had been lying in wait for it.

When I read that the Marines were recruiting something called combat correspondents, I wrote asking to be one. My son had just been born when my draft notice came in March 1943; there was a grace period of a few months, and in November I entered the Marine Corps and was sent, jammed together with hundreds in an antiquated train, for boot training to Parris Island, South Carolina.

That experience was the next gift laid at my feet by the father of all things, war: bringing me close, again, to the kind of kids I had left when we parted on graduation evening from high school; and an acceptance together with them into what I saw as a harsh and spiritual unity. Stripped of higher education, of past, and of future ambitions for myself, I was becoming one of the anonymous many. I was happy.

At nearly thirty, I saw myself preparing to advance side by side with these new comrades—eighteen-, nineteen-, and twenty-year-olds—into war's mist. I reacted with fond obedience to the playfully brutal routines of boot camp.

I tried to do everything the way others did. I was part of a totality and felt a great collective will working on me and shaping me.

At the same time, I knew it was really a ceremony of initiation, first step toward laying my life "on freedom's altar"—words I had written before this all began.

On the rifle range, there was the shock of excitement as the rifle recoiled. There was pride at how well I had shot—I, who had never even seen a rifle close up—and at how swiftly I fieldstripped mine. There was quiet satisfaction as we marched, stinging in winter cold, our classy Marine boondockers kicking up dust, to the "Awn-hup awn-hup awn-hup yer lef" drone of the drill instructor.

I must have succeeded completely in taking on the identity of the boot Marine. Our platoon had stood inspection well. Our junior drill instructor made us stand at attention in front of our bunks. We stood, arms stiff, chests thrown out, legs spread slightly, stomachs in.

After ten minutes of hushed, tense silence, he spoke: "You cocksuckers. You stupid pricks. You clowns and bastards. You fuckers. You're a fucking good inspection platoon."

"Thank you, sir!" as one we thirty-nine chorused.

I was pierced by the beauty of the playing of taps.

The bugle faltered, as usual, strained at the last high note, but fell back. It didn't matter, for all the togetherness in utter loneliness of this life I loved so much as I strove and endured it, drifted on the notes high and higher into emptiness.

"End of an iron day," I wrote proudly to my wife that evening, seated on the footlocker that contained everything in my new life.

I smelled the steaming smell of dungarees soaked by a sudden rain, drying. One of the guys, Henry, squatted at the foot of the stove, beating his off-key guitar and droning in the reedy nasal minor voice of a mountaineer:

Not far from me
They's an ole holler tree
Where you lay down a dollar or two

An' you go round the bend
An' you come back again
With a jug of that ole mountain dew.

Only once was there an intrusion into the self-enclosed adventure on which all my inner strength and imagination were locked. I stared at a newspaper clipping a man in our platoon got in a letter from the outside world.

Nearly a thousand Marines had died storming a Pacific island—Tarawa. Intelligence was faulty, the landing boats struck coral far from the beach, and men were drowned or shot down trying to wade in through surf too deep for them.

A gallant Marine victory. But—

Nearly a thousand!

A dark intruder had suddenly brushed against our charmed boot camp world. I saw I was not the only one who felt that thrill I recognized as fear. I did not talk about it, and few did. We decided it had to be dismissed. We went back to our "Flank and wheel," our "Rip-march rip-march rip-march," our stripping of our rifles, our stacking of them, our comradeship as we prepared ourselves.

From boot camp most of my platoon were shipped to Camp Lejeune for more harsh training. Unlike me, they would be line infantrymen, thrown into mortal risk over and over again. I was detailed to Washington, to the Marine Corps's PR office, and made a sergeant—combat correspondent as promised. I had a few weeks with my wife and baby son, and to parade around in my greens and be admired. It was all very unfair, and I knew it.

When I was sent west, I knew again I was fortunate. There would be no long, demoralizing months waiting in stateside camps.

Still, for a few weeks at Camp Pendleton, near San Diego, there was nothing to do all day between liberties. Some of the men shot craps on the barracks floor. There was no drill, no training, not even morning roll call. I forgot everything I had learned about fieldstripping my rifle.

On liberty, we would go into town and get drunk and try for pickups. I found out I was untalented.

I did meet a girl Marine, and it was a tender, sweet, and brief experience. I was married and refused to lie. Didn't even have the decency to say I was separated.

There were ten of us combat correspondents in the barracks together. We were angry at the delay and could not wait to get to where there was battle.

One day four of us were playing desultory basketball on an outdoor court—one on one, long shot and follow-up. We suddenly stopped playing, gathered in the center of the court, and decided we had to get out of there.

We marched resolutely through the bright sun and camp dust to headquarters and asked to see the CO. We were bold and definite. "We were sent out as combat correspondents. Our general back there is waiting for our dispatches from combat."

Either in bewilderment or in determination to shove it up and hear us cry, the CO said he would think it over. Two days later, orders came. We were marched to the San Diego docks, panting under the weight of our seabags, and loaded unceremoniously into a destroyer escort. By nightfall we were rocking in the Pacific, trying to hold our food down.

It was a small crew-packed ship, and we were unexpected additions. We hot-bunked—using a sack when a sailor got up to go on watch or on duty, and giving it back when he needed it. The rest of the time we squatted in the narrow aisles between the bunks, or in the galley, or on the oily deck.

The little destroyer escort bounded like a cork. I was proud of being the only one of the ten who till the end could still clamber to the galley for chow. I even made my way back with soup for one fellow correspondent, Harold Breard. That just annoyed him—he would turn his head away.

But the stars, the constellations!

They would be the endless backdrop for the myth called the war, which was finally beginning.

At Pearl Harbor we were transferred to a different kind of vessel altogether.

Suddenly we were out of the world of oily decks, foul-smelling narrow bunks beneath ceilings too low to straighten up, and gorge rising as the tin can leaped and fell back into wave troughs. Suddenly we were swathed in the soft calm air of the South Pacific, lolling on soft clean individual cots on the wide, intensely clean polished deck, sliding along over a sparkling ocean, under brilliant yet mild sun and soft nodding night stars, amid crates of ice-cold oranges, huge lockers bursting with steaks, tons of ice cream, all dished out to crew and to us—honored sole passengers aboard that refrigeration ship, rear echelon of rear echelons, sailing as if forever, in a world in which there could never possibly be any war.

An unreal voyage. But by this time we were taking anything in stride.

And one rose-flushed morning, just as suddenly, the refrigeration ship stood in a pure lapis lazuli lagoon circled with shining coral atolls, behind which we saw high palms. "Eniwetok," said a sailor.

Only those who saw Eniwetok before it became an atomic experiment can imagine the purity of that water and those skies. I could not believe such forlorn splendor existed in this world. We had been allowed to enter a secret domain of palms, white sand, and coral branches in looking-glass water.

I knew perfectly well that Americans and Japanese had died less than a year ago on that atoll, and were still buried there, but I could not believe it. It was theory, rumor, while this unearthly beauty was fact.

We must have climbed down into a craft with some sailors to bathe near the edge of the coral. As I stood in the transparent water I felt privileged beyond all others, owning for a moment this world of coral and sky and sun. I could see my feet, down to each separate toe, clearly and sharply. The bright nakedness of my body through the utterly clear green-blue water heightened the illusion of being granted entry into an untrammeled and magical part of the universe.

Dazed, we climbed back aboard the refrigeration ship, at anchor in Eniwetok lagoon, in time for our steak supper.

That mid-June evening, listening with bemused detachment to news of the world's hurly-burly outside our magic lagoon, we heard the refrigeration ship's radio telling about a battle that had begun on some island called Saipan, in the Marianas. We sighed. We were too late for that. We would have to go on, for a while, roaming the Pacific on our charmed ship.

Still, we must have protested, weakly. And lo! at nightfall we were put on a motor launch with our seabags. We landed amid high palms on the white beach and straggled into a quonset hut. We would have the atoll and its lagoon at our disposal for a while, as solace for the missed battle.

An hour later they were snatched from us.

We had demanded from the duty officer in his quonset hut "the next available transport to Saipan." He obliged us.

In the dead of the Pacific night I clung to the back rail of a motorboat bobbing frantically across the lagoon, headed toward a dark hull at its farthest point near the outlet. I hung on grimly, too excited to be terrified, my double pack with the Hermes typewriter on one side trying to hurl me off backward into the ocean.

The motorboat managed to pull up, a rope ladder was let down, one by one we climbed and then were dragged up over the ship's rail, and found ourselves packed shoulder to shoulder with three thousand replacement Marines on a transport headed for Saipan.

*The strange thing is that this
is a beautiful island . . . but
now it is a terrible place.*

2–Island of the Dead

Out of the vast empty ocean, suddenly, there was Saipan.

It was shaped like a coolie's hat, that climbed to a mountain peak. It was dark green and light green, and girdled by
reefs on which small white waves broke, curling. Beside it,
a low-lying, less rugged, and more verdant sister island,
Tinian, rose from the gray-blue water.

In front of Saipan our ships covered the ocean. They were
shelling the island while our planes dive-bombed. This was
an innocent, bright panorama before us. Kept at a distance,
it was magnificent. The shells flew over us and approached
the clay-colored buildings of a town. I could hear—and thought
I could actually see—them split the air in their passage. Then
pretty, harmless flames spurted where they landed in the

town, over which smoke climbed and climbed. It was hard to believe this meant the town was burning.

On a line across the island, two Marine divisions and an Army division were killing and being killed. But for us, for a short while, this could remain a thing of beauty: the island standing calmly in the sea, with its seawall of shallows drawing an oval of light green and white about it—a painting done in a tranquil era, by an unknown master. The burning town was an added bright touch, in far perspective, to provide contrast. This beauty was balanced by a barely restrained fright. We guessed that dreadful things might be occurring behind the pretty picture. Yet fright in turn was held in check by awe and fascination. We stood packed against the rail three deep, staring.

A heavy plane whirred low over the transport, zooming by our massed upturned faces. "It's our bomber!" "Look at the son of a bitch go!"—there was time to yell. A few seconds later, at medium distance, came a low, deep thump. The bomber was in fact Japanese, one of the few that had reached Saipan. Its pilot must have realized too late what a target we made, and a few seconds later he let his bomb go into the prow of a ship down the line. After that we were ordered below decks, and three thousand men scrambled down— which would have helped a lot if another bomb had hit.

Next came real, sinking-in fright, as we were unloaded from the transport and then loaded onto trucks that rumbled past debris of battle: dead oxen, their legs sticking up over bloated bellies, and then in the fields an overlooked human body. The truck was jolting in time to the uneven thump of artillery rounds—like physical shocks hitting us. They were from our guns, but we did not know that.

I only knew, all at once, that I was surrounded by violent danger, random death. The ten combat correspondents in the truck sat as if catatonic. There was, we all suddenly understood, another and terrifying dimension.

* * *

The landings had succeeded, with heavy Marine losses. The 2nd and 4th Marine divisions, joined by the 27th Army division, spaced out across the island and drove north, destroying Japanese forces, taking local counterattacks, and awaiting the final big one.

Japanese reinforcements had managed to land, but the ships carrying their artillery, ammunition, and spare parts had been scattered by storm and sunk by American submarines. Charges, for all the brave screams of "Banzai!", had to be carried out partly with bayonets mounted on bamboo sticks.

The decision in battle had been sealed by the time I got there. What remained was to sacrifice enough lives to finish Saipan's conquest.

The combat correspondents and photographers settled in the captured town of Charan Kanoa in a big wooden and stucco house, once an official residence. It had been hit by our artillery. The rattan screens over its doorways and huge square windows had been destroyed, and it stood with gaping openings—a dirty white skeleton of a building.

The basic job of the combat correspondents was to write "Joe Blow" stories, which were sent to the hometown papers of the Marines. Joe Blow was the enlisted foot Marine, a figure who stood for all the foot Marines.

There was fondness in this moniker, and also pride. Its trace of disdain was mainly the self-disdain of the line fighter in all ages who knows his duty is to be expendable, to win for his commanders, and who sees through both his commanders and himself.

The Army had its GI Joes, made familiar by Mauldin's cartoon characters Willie and Joe. These figures had the same elements of fondness and disdain. Their representation and humor, however, were tailored to the mass of Americans of a wide age-span from whom the Army came; while the subjects of our dispatches were an unsophisticated elite—an elite only in their greater readiness to be sent into attack.

If there was—and I believe there was—a difference between us combat correspondents and the reporters for *Stars and Stripes*, part of it was the difference between Army and Marines. And part was because of our dual role as we were told to understand it—as journalists and also as plain enlisted infantry Marines. This was symbolized by the dual nature of our battle gear: M-1 rifle (the same one I had carried in boot camp, packed in cosmoline and shipped ahead of me) and baby Hermes typewriter in half the pack.

Whatever else we typed in our dispatches, our first responsibility was not to focus on "the big picture" but on the individual Marine: we were the bards recruited to sing the deeds of the Joe Blows. Drafting men with media backgrounds and connections for this purpose was a brilliant and practical idea carried out under Robert Denig, the general in charge of public relations.

The *Stars and Stripes* reporters, and civilians assigned to the Pacific, also sent in stories about the men; but I believe our relationship with the Joe Blows, our fellow foot Marines, was more intimate. Most of the combat correspondents were assigned to the line regiments, as I would be later. The dual definition of our job gave it a special aura and made us able to partake of the Marine infantry's mystique.

There were anomalies in our position, and sometimes I envied the civilian correspondents with their "assimilated" rank of lieutenant-colonel. But nothing is perfect.

In our dispatches, the customary way to refer to the Japanese was "Japs." It was convenient—it took longer to type "Japanese." Sometimes "Nips" (for Nipponese) was used. I was disquieted by "Japs," probably because I was more alert to any hint of racism, because of my Russian-Jewish origins, than were some of the others. Still, I also used "Japs."

At the gutted house in Charan Kanoa I pulled out the baby
Hermes I had carried eleven thousand miles in my pack,
along with the extra socks, the extra skivvy tops and draw-
ers, a set of watercolor paints I had bought in San Diego on
an impulse, typing paper, notebooks, glasses that I didn't
need, and an album of photos of my year-old son that could
fit into my dungaree pocket. Sitting on a box in that skeleton of a building I typed stories from penciled notes. Our PR
officer, a captain named John Popham who had been a reporter
with the *New York Times*, sent the stories on.

Popham and I were very different. His humor was not my
style, and I had never lived easily with anyone in authority.
Still, he was fair enough in his dealings with me and others.
He felt responsibility, but he didn't often bother us.

I typed a stream of Joe Blow stories about 2d Division
Marines:

About a kid from Richland Center, Wisconsin, graduate
of the local high school, who had gone into violent action
with a mortar unit on D-day. The story was directed to the
Richland Center Democrat. (The kid himself asked me urgently
to please send it there.)

About two young Marines who told me Saipan was worse
than Tarawa had been: "It's because here you have time to
think. At Tarawa you didn't."

About a Hispanic American amtrac driver from Los Ange-
les and his two Anglo assistant drivers, whom he taught
enough Spanish so they agreed to name their lumbering iron
mount "Boca del Muerte"—Mouth of Death. "That D-day,
Mouth of Death sure went into the mouth of hell," one of the
young Anglo Marines told me.

About a Japanese soldier charging a Marine's foxhole and
hurling a grenade ahead of him. The Marine had no time to
react; but the grenade hit an overhanging tree limb, which
like a baseball bat sent it back at the onrushing infantryman,

blowing off his head. The headless body plunged into the Marine's foxhole.

Many of the stories the men told were like that last one—about single happenings that stood out, sometimes traumatic, sometimes incongruously funny or inexplicable, from the haze and maze of combat. Those were the ones, I guessed, that would be remembered forever.

I had not yet shared any of their experiences, but was determined I would.

Wandering around around Charan Kanoa, I inspected its smashed buildings open to the warm rain, its remnants of thatched roofs consumed by our bombardments. Vaguely I understood that much had been destroyed and that we had done it. Wooden bowls, chopsticks, schoolbooks showing Japanese children saluting the rising-sun flag or watching their emperor ride past, sepia photos of naked Japanese babies, and booklets extolling that jewel in the empire's crown, Saipan, all lay pell-mell in the yards and the streets and the fields outside town—evidence of frantic flight.

I picked up—and sent a dispatch about—the many scattered handbooks with notes in Japanese explaining earnestly how to read English poetry to distill its beauty. There was a broken Japanese recording of "Bei mir bist du schane" and a torn Japanese edition of *Mein Kampf*. But German sway over Saipan had ended with World War I, and in the twenty-five years since then it had become a Japanese island. This was clear from the remains of its identity strewn everywhere around me. In the field outside town I found a ragged doll with a pretty Japanese face. I snatched it up for a souvenir then threw it down again, angry at myself.

I set out one afternoon in a jeep with a civilian correspondent from the *Baltimore Sun*. He wanted to visit the Army division's sector. I agreed, wondering if the Marine

Corps would distribute Joe Blow stories about Army GIs.

We bounced across a sugarcane field and into a grassy clearing where, behind a row of saplings, a platoon of one of the companies of the 27th was deployed. They sprawled on the grass, not dug in but in a perimeter of sorts. It looked as if a decision had just been made to stay there for the night.

We headed for the platoon lieutenant and got his OK to talk to some of the men. We walked among them and started getting names and hometown addresses. The civilian correspondent was looking for men from Baltimore. I hoped to find someone from Cleveland but would settle for any place.

They were mostly young, though not as young as our Marines. Their army boots were clumsy, not like the beautiful leather boondockers we Marines wore. Their dungarees were more slouchy than ours. They were quiet—more quiet, I thought, than Marines would have been.

In the surprisingly pale light of the sun—now low, filtering through those saplings—I watched a big, strongly built man stride into the platoon's area. The platoon leader came up, and the big man pointed and talked, exuding confidence. He finished talking and strode past us.

Turning back to the GIs, I saw their eyes following the company commander.

"That's Tiger Hill," one of them said. There was pride in his voice. "He's a powerful fighter. Ain't afraid of nothing."

A couple of the men sprawled nearby chimed in. "We'll be all right, with Tiger Hill," one of them assured another, and me as well.

I squatted down beside one of the GIs. A thin, handsome youth, he lay on the grass, hands clasped behind his head, relaxed—no, it was more like being quietly, sadly accepting. He was from Brooklyn. I told him I was from Cleveland, and just the fact that each of us was from a town the other knew about established some rapport.

As I jotted down his words, I thought about how all of them seemed subdued, buoyed only by their confidence in the invincibility of Captain Tiger Hill. He was now striding off toward the next platoon, and the young Brooklyn soldier's eyes turned to follow him.

The *Baltimore Sun* correspondent called over to me and motioned toward our jeep. The driver was standing beside it, waiting. It was then I sensed that the light had been waning, the sky turning green behind the copse of saplings, and there was a sudden coolness in the air.

There was enough of a bond already with these men for me to sense that they would like it if I stayed and dug in with them. It would be a kind of extra reassurance. I hesitated, but climbed up from my position on one knee and fumbled to put my notebook into my dungaree pocket. "Well, so long," I said. "I've got a story to do." Then, "Good luck." On the ride back to Charan Kanoa, the two of us talked about how we couldn't hang around, how our job was to get the stories and file them.

That night the long-awaited counterattack came, hitting the sector of the 27th where I had been and a sector held by the 9th Marines. It swept over several companies before being broken up by supporting troops. By the end of the next day the last of the attackers had been destroyed, or had killed themselves, and in the cane fields sailors from our ships were frisking their bodies and cutting off ears for souvenirs.

That company of the 27th had been overrun. A Marine bivouac had also been overrun, some men caught in their camouflage tents. The weather had turned blazing hot, and by the time I walked through there the bodies were all blackened and greatly bloated, with huge black swollen mouths thickly ringed by great sugarcane flies. They lay like slaughtered, decomposing cattle, or monstrous black flowers.

Back in the PR house, we talked mostly about how the Japanese had been halted by Marine gunners who depressed the muzzles of their 75s to fire point-blank.

I filed no story about my visit to that company of the 27th.

The burial of a combat photographer, killed when he went up to a forward position during that counterattack, was put into a letter home that somehow got past the censors. I changed the names of both the man and his buddy:

Bodies could now be recovered. About noon, we learned McLean's had been found. The captain he had gone up with had also been killed—a big, strong-cursing, jovial man, popular with the other officers at division headquarters. A truck was bringing the two bodies back to Charan Kanoa.

We went down to the division cemetery. I barely dragged myself along the dust-choked road. The sun was heavy, the air seemed filled with maggots. Acrid decay was everywhere, and a physical and mental lethargy pressed our limbs and made us hardly able to move. In the cemetery, on either side of us, they were unloading bodies from six-by-six trucks. The air here was even heavier, and rank. The sun was merciless, and exhausting. A six-by-six came bouncing and swerving toward where we stood, by the hole which had been dug. A head could be seen bobbing inside, the head of a man sitting inside the six-by-six, with the bodies. It was McLean's buddy, little Spink. He was bareheaded, and his eyes and face were enflamed. As the truck jolted by us, he leaned his head over the side, and vomited. The truck swerved and started backing up. His head stayed bent over the side, and he kept vomiting, thin gruelly vomit. As the truck turned its backside to us, I saw the back flap was down, and the two bodies lay crosswise, one over the other, on the floor. They were too big to be the bodies of men. They were like the bodies of steers. Some men of the graves registration detail clambered into the truck, and took hold of the bodies and yanked them toward the back where the flap was down. They dropped them to the ground, onto stretchers which had been brought and put there. They were indeed great, swollen beyond life-size. McLean was recognizable though his face was bloated and the sugar flies had settled in his ears, his mouth and his nostrils. The graves registration men bent under the weight as they brought the stretchers to the long gaping hole dug in the earth. The chaplain, a young man with a face ravaged with uncertainty, read something out of his Bible. They turned the stretchers upside down in a practiced, expert way, and McLean and the captain, together, rolled into the depth. All this time, little Spink's head bobbed over the side of the six-by-six, as he vomited and retched without end.

The man who had driven the six-by-six was standing beside me. He looked up at Spink and then at me, and explained, "Saki."

Sorrow or saki, saki or sorrow, he had shepherded his buddy all the way from where he had been found.

June moved into July on Saipan. The heat, the sugarcane flies, and the constant bursts of warm rain made slogging up to the companies of the 2d Division harder. That, and the sense that others were giving and risking so much more than I was, dragged me down. The long lines of filled ambulance jeeps bumping past me going the other way, bound for the division field hospital—the eyes of desperately wounded sometimes open and fixed, as if on me—were an accusation.

I had written Joe Blow stories about the transportation unit, so it was easy for me to commandeer a jeep. The driver, his buddy, and I set out toward one of the companies but were soon lost, turning this way and that along mountainous roads. We stopped at a crossing of two paths, with nothing but trees in sight, one path leading up and the other down.

"We'll be all right," the eighteen-year-old buddy assured the eighteen-year-old driver. "Levin always knows how to get us back on track." I realized, astonished, that I was a comforting figure to them, the colorful veteran correspondent, and I shuddered.

"This way," I finally said. We took the path leading down, and it swerved, bringing the jeep to the edge of a forest pool in which a dozen naked Japanese were bathing. They looked up at us. We looked at them.

"Prisoners," I explained, hoping this was so. My driver hesitated, turned the wheel, and got us out of there, and a few minutes later we stumbled into a bivouac of Marines.

The marriage between Marines and Army for the campaign was not an easy one. In the PR house we heard there were shouting matches between generals. The Marines, filled with teenagers who when they started had no idea of death, believed in driving ahead, losing however many had to be lost, and gaining objectives quickly. The Army, with somewhat older—some quite a lot older—men, liked to advance cautiously and methodically, preserving lives. The Marines said this broke the advancing line, opening up flanks, and cost as much or more over longer time.

I was proud of the Marine way of doing things, but somewhere in me I treacherously agreed with the Army.

Overwhelmed by experiences, impressions, and the heat, I stopped going up. Whatever derring-do had made me march up to the colonel at Pendleton and demand to be shipped to where there was combat had seeped out of me.

Men on the line still lay in mud-filled foxholes or in gullies, tensing at every movement in front of them. But I settled down in the remains of that house taken over by the PR captain and started on a monumental allegorical painting of Saipan, using those watercolor paints I had dragged from the States in my pack.

The others stared but said nothing; most of us were characters, each in his own way. Into my primitive painting I put all the terror and heroism I had felt: a gallant Marine stood astride that beautiful, terrible island.

At the island's extremity, Marpi Point, Japanese civilians—men, boys, women with children in their arms—were throwing themselves off the high cliffs, to smash against the rocks below. I made no move to go up there.

But soon after, in those last Saipan days, in pouring rain, I came out of my shocked state and played poker with the other combat correspondents and photographers. *Life*'s photographer, the very gifted Gene Smith, and one of the other civilians joined in.

Some of the men kept bluffing, building the pots up and forcing out others who had good hands but couldn't risk huge losses. I argued eloquently that this cut down on the role of skill and spoiled our fun. The others, struck by my moral exhortation, agreed to cut down on the bluffing.

On almost the next hand, I picked up a straight flush; could hardly believe it; put the cards face down, peeked again hastily, and bid. It was quite a pot by the time the last of the others sighed, put down his three kings, and said, "It's yours, Levin." Proudly I laid out my cards.

It was not quite a straight flush, or any kind of flush. I had taken an eight of hearts for a seven of diamonds. Nobody trusted me or would play with me after that.

I finished my epic watercolor.

Then, on the day the island was secured I typed a final dispatch, aimed not at any hometown paper's city editor but at anybody in the universe who would listen.

SAIPAN, JULY 11—(Delayed)—This is an island of the dead.

Its area is about 75 square miles. Seldom have so many perished in violence during so short a time in so small a space.

The great majority of the killed were Japanese, but many were American soldiers and Marines.

The dead are everywhere. They lie in their strained postures of death in the burnt cane fields, in ditches, in foxholes, in the beds of small streams, on the hillsides and mountain slopes. They float face down in the sea until the slow tide washes them onto the beach. They lie buried in blasted buildings and in dynamited caves.

They lie in numbered rows in the cemeteries. Trucks follow one another with their sorrowful blanket-covered loads.

The fighting was frantic and without mercy. A wounded Marine captain is finished with a bayonet thrust through the throat. Five Japanese are cornered in a cave among the roots of a huge banyan tree; one wants to surrender, the others refuse to let him out; there is nothing to be done—a Marine flamethrower chars them all. A group of Japanese civilians approaches a group of Marines, as if to surrender. Suddenly they part and run aside, revealing the rifles of Japanese troops behind them. One Marine is slain, others wounded. The rest leave no enemy alive. In another area, with knives and bayonets fastened to the ends of bamboo poles, the Japanese charge into machine gun and rifle fire. The charge is stopped. Those who remain alive put grenades to their chests and pull the pins. Others plunge special hara-kiri knives into their bowels. Others use swords. Women and children are slain by the soldiers when our troops draw near. Then the soldiers make a last hopeless banzai charge. Tanks and Marine infantry move carefully and relentlessly through the cane fields, flushing the Japanese out like rabbits and killing them. Japanese ambush parties fall on small groups of men moving up to and from the front, kill or wound them, and are cornered and killed in turn. Sleeping Marines are butchered in their shelter tents. The Japanese who have made the sortie are sealed off and methodically destroyed.

In each area of 100 or 200 yards where the Marines or Army pushed ahead during the previous day, or where the Japanese made a banzai counterattack, the smell of death is sweet and heavy.

New names are etched in biting acid into American remembrance. Each is where American lives bled into the green and reddish earth of Saipan. Green Beach and Yellow Beach and Red Beach and Blue Beach and Jap Beach—the awful beachheads. Mount Tapotchau, on whose slopes hundreds died. Sugar Loaf. Dead Man's Hill. Hell's Pocket. Flame-tree Hill. Watchtower Hill. Garapan. Marpi Point. Each for hundreds a memory that separates them from all other men—a bitterness for killed comrades and a thrilling echo of terror and struggle that they can communicate to no one.

"I don't think there's a square foot of this island that somebody didn't die on," said an Army tank captain.

The same thought was spoken again and again. Nobody can fail to recognize and be awed by this island of the dead.

The strange thing is that this is a beautiful island. The sea close to the beaches is shallow, light green, and warm. Further out it is steel blue or Prussian blue. The flame-trees are garish and profuse with delicate flowers. There are mountain shrines and temples. There are banyan trees, banana trees and papaya trees. The evening sky is rose and mauve, and the air is gentle. Mount Tapotchau is a mountain out of a Japanese tapestry.

But now it is a terrible place.

Two love birds circle around the cliff
  (Above Tinian Town, above Tinian Town)
The sky is pale blue and poison-green
  And the flame-tree flowers drift down, drift down

A young rifleman sprawls in the cane
  With arms flung back (and the flowers drift down)
And his buddies move out and take the cliff
  Above Tinian Town, above Tinian Town

3—We and They

There was less than a mile of ocean between Saipan and Tinian. It would not be a difficult landing. Only remnants of the Japanese forces were there, with hardly any artillery and no more planes. Their last, based on Tinian, had made a few bombing runs on Saipan before being killed by our fighters.

I had resolved to be in on the landing but did not pull the right strings. I could not get space in an LCVP until D plus 1, and after an interminable choppy ride, with hours of night circling and waiting, we landed as dawn was breaking. The beach was secure.

As I climbed off the beach onto high ground, the morning's dead were laid out in parallel rows, on stretchers their blood had soaked spongy, under green blankets. On the wide black borders of the blankets their names—or the names of those who originally got the blankets—were stenciled. The black borders furled over them like broad bands of mourning.

But the landing was going to be easy! I was stunned. For them—I stood in front of eight—it had been final.

The idea that these men were no longer in my universe was suddenly offensive, unacceptable. I stood watching them for a few minutes, outraged, without coherent thoughts, and then went on. Nearby in a long winding trench a whole platoon of Japanese lay, one neatly behind the other, slaughtered by machine gun fire as they slogged faithfully toward the beach to shore up defenses that no longer existed. My feelings about that sight I put aside. They did not belong. It was enough to feel for our dead; to take on more would have been too much.

I walked across the island, catching on with one outfit and then another in the sweep aimed at the island's only town, at its opposite end. I don't know who bestowed on it the name Tinian Town; I may have been the one. The music of the name wove itself into my image of the island.

We crossed a strangely quiet, strangely vacant airfield, passing only three or four smashed Japanese bombers still in their bays. We walked across the airfield quietly, as if not wanting to disturb its abandoned somnolence.

The next couple of nights I sacked in with a rocket unit, whose missiles would hurtle with a grinding roar into the high ground in front of Tinian Town. I took notes for stories, took my turn at the perimeter's machine gun at night, and other times slept under the platform on which the rockets were mounted. As the night deepened, yellow Japanese flares and white Marine flares would rise, burn brilliantly and mysteriously, and then fade. Thick darkness crept up, stiffness grasped the bones, rain plopped inside one's dungaree combat jacket, down spine and thighs. In the cane field beyond, a figure moved. Ours? Theirs? Nothing happens, all is well. At last, a pale soggy morning emerged.

In the early morning and evening, I would hear the cooing of mourning doves—love birds. And once I glimpsed a pair of them circling together above the distant trees. That soft and plaintive music seemed out of another reality, a counterpoint to everything we were involved in.

A day later, near the bluffs in front of Tinian Town, there was a one-sided firefight. Firing out of a cave on the bluff, Japanese riflemen killed two Marines. I was in the group that spread out on the low ground and fired into the mouth of the cave. Finally a Marine clawed up the bluff from the side, worked his way toward the cave, and hurled in a grenade. That should have finished it.

Unbelieving, I saw a form spring from the cave and start scrambling up the side of the bluff. We seemed to leap forward, rifles trained on that desperate thing; we were like furious animals after prey flushed from hiding. We fired in a kind of delirium, and the man—not a thing or a fugitive animal but a fellow man, I suddenly realized, horrified—fell forward on the bluff and lay spread-eagled, arms out and forward, legs back, like a five-pointed star on the slope.

Even as I felt this horror at myself, I knew it was a device for taking the curse off my eager joy at being the hunter.

The two Marines who had been killed lay face up, heads slightly down, in a depression or shellhole that must have been their too-shallow foxhole. They were two beautiful young men, sprawled against each other, one with his arms flung back the way children (my child too) sometimes sleep, but with his bright blue eyes open as if accusing me.

This sight wove itself with the sound of the mourning doves that had cooed in the woods, with the musical sound of "Tinian Town," and with the shaking effect the firefight just ended had on me. That night I wrote in my notebook the short poem that opens this chapter.

I knew of no other way to pay homage to those beautiful youths for whom time and space had ended. I could not send a Joe Blow story—I could not transmit their names. One of the combat photographers could have been asked to take a shot of the scene, but it would only have gone into Marine Corps files. Our public could take news of deaths, but a close-up photo of those slain young men, without good reason to run it, would not help the war effort.

It was ironic that one of my more successful dispatches came from an incident that must have taken place on the afternoon of the same day. Even some of the Marine cast was the same. This story got distribution although it named no Joe Blows, and it would appear in an anthology of combat correspondents' stories.

The Marines were standing outside the wire-enclosed stockade and the Japanese women, children and old men were inside the enclosure. One Marine, just returned from the front lines, squatted and beckoned to a Japanese child who was sitting on the ground with a woman, presumably his mother. The stocky kid, about four or five, wearing a Jap soldier's cap, came bustling forward. He stopped at the wire and stood foursquare, his legs firmly set and wide apart, his eyes level with the Marine's.

The Marine reached into his dungaree pocket for a bar of chocolate, broke it in half and dropped one piece into the cupped outstretched palms of the child. The boy stiffened, clutching the chocolate in one hand, and with mature dignity bowed quickly, wheeled, and raced back to the woman who was sitting on the grass.

It was the bow that got the other Marines who were standing around. They had just returned from a firefight and had seen several of their mates killed and badly wounded. They were dark-eyed, bearded, dirty and tired. But when the Jap kid bowed their eyes lightened and they moved nearer the stockade.

A photographer focused his movie camera while a sec-

ond Marine broke off a piece of chocolate and went up
to the wire. Instantly the Jap kid bustled forward again,
grave and courteous, but obviously confident. The second Marine, a Mexican who wore a long handlebar mus-
tache, looked like a tougher, wilier Trader Horn. The Jap
child and Trader Horn regarded one another seriously for
a moment. The boy proffered his cupped palms, and the
Marine placed the chocolate in them. The camera ground.
The boy made his jerky bow and raced back with his second triumph.

He was tried a third time, but there was no more
K-ration chocolate; so a third Marine advanced with some
Japanese candy drops. The camera was set. The Marines
stood with rapt faces, and the Marine who was offering
the candy beckoned. The boy came charging forward, his
brown hands stretched out. The candy was dropped into
them. And then the boy turned and raced back, without
a bow! Everybody began to laugh.

"The little bastard!"

"He's learning fast!"

"His own candy ain't worth it. He wants that K-ration!"

Everybody was laughing and kidding, the Japanese
women in Japanese, the Marines in English. Everybody
knew the kid had crossed everybody up by not bowing.

One of the Marines, who had been fighting in the cane
field that morning, suddenly got mad, and bitter.

"Don't forget what you saw out there this morning," he
said. "Don't forget it."

Trader Horn said, "Those kids didn't have anything to
do with it. Or these women."

"I hate the bastards. I say kill them all. Don't forget those
two Marines with their heads all bloody."

"That's two different things," the first Marine protested.

"What happened out there hasn't got anything to do
with what's going on here," Trader Horn backed him.

"I wouldn't mind having that little kid for my kid brother," a third Marine said defiantly.

"Out there," Trader Horn said, "we kill them or they kill us but now it's over and they're the same people we are. Look at that little son of a bitch."

They'd found some more Japanese candy and the child came rushing out again, like a star player rushing back into the game. Everybody waited to see if he would bow this time. His mother had been coaching him. The guns were booming hollowly a couple of miles away, but nobody heard the guns.

Late in August, Saipan and Tinian were declared secure. The tense excitement, and our comradeship in fear and resolve, were over. It was a good time to harvest Joe Blow stories—I could be pretty sure the men I wrote about would be alive to get clippings from home. But I felt played out, and it was hard to muster enthusiasm.

By the first of September, with all of what had happened still like a dark half-developed print inside me, I was on the Pearl Harbor–bound troopship. I didn't do much thinking. I jotted down notes of what the men said as they lay on their bunks, or squatted in the aisles, or leaned up against the rail watching the phosphorescence blazing in the night waters purling past by moonlight.

They talked about how it would be back at the base: about the waiting piles of letters; about women if they were lucky and got liberty in Honolulu; about the huge steak with eggs they would order, with beer, at a restaurant there. They also talked about curious Saipan and Tinian experiences.

"So I crawled down into the fucking cave, wondering why I was risking my fucking butt, and got that Jap baby and crawled back out of that fucking cave, expecting a fucking bullet in my fucking back. . . ."

"One a them ran for it and we drilled him, but then we

sent this guy that gave up back in there and he jabbered at the other two fuckers and they gave up. I nearly shit I was so relieved."

"Fuck no, Ski didn't get it. He only got a fucking crease, but it was the third fucking one. He's fucking stateside by now, fuck yes."

(The all-purpose word for any Marine was "fuck"; it had not yet dripped into the American mainstream. In my novel, written soon after the war, I agonized over it and—urged by two editors—changed it to "muck." Mailer, in his novel, hit on "fugg." Years later, preparing a new edition in a postmodern age, I painstakingly changed every "muck" back to "fuck.")

They also talked about buddies who got it, and about why some guys got it and some didn't. It was a great mystery that troubled everyone, myself included. As the days and nights passed, there were longer silences.

The troop holds were dimly lit. We hated going down into the heavy air. Climbing over battle gear, we made our way to our sacks. Naked limbs, thrust out from the sacks into the narrow aisles, were strangely white.

In a corner at the far end of the hold, a young tenor sang quietly, over and over—

Fuck 'em *all*
Fuck 'em *all*
The long, the short,
And the tall. . . .

Also on this return voyage, standing on the swaying deck, I suddenly wrote another poem in my notebook. This one surprised me. Its key thought was that "Nothing is lost or is gained"—that there is

Nothing but sunrise and sunsetting
Men fighting the things that are—
Birthgiving and bloodletting
And a drunk god snoring afar.

I did not like what I had written. It was too bleak and too cynical. But poetry, like dreams, often sees and tells us things
we do not want to hear or see.

Three times a day we stood in the ship-long chow line,
climbed down the hatch into the blazing-hot galley, stuffed
in food standing like animals with sweat pouring down us,
and climbed back up.

The stars swayed over us. The sun rose and set. The days,
the weeks, and the routine did their work. Memories were
erased, or toned down till men could live with them. By the
time we neared our base Saipan, island of the dead, was
behind us, as was its sister Tinian, island of the young Marine
lying with arms flung back while the flowers drifted down.
And there was nothing surprising about being alive, and
being able to enjoy life.

How or where exactly I first ran into Joe Berger I can't
recall. It was not on the returning troopship. Probably it was
at our base on Oahu, Camp Catlin. I see him coming down
the path toward me, his feet out at a Chaplinesque angle,
his pisscutter almost equally awry, his kind eyes staring from
behind thick un-Marine glasses. At the first meeting, Joe
struck me as the stereotype of the unwarlike, unathletic, tal-
mudistic Jew—a stereotype I had consciously avoided in my
life. I not only wondered why he was in that (badly fitted)
Marine uniform at all, but was reluctant to become friends
with him.

As I got to know him and his attitude toward our warrior
trade, I also felt my decision to be a heroic, rifle-toting,
battle-relishing Marine was being challenged. And I feared
some of his absolute rejection of machismo would rub off on
me. Proximity to him might rouse the impulse to be thoughtful, and to take less seriously the Marine legend so central
to my present life.

This traitorous tendency was also part of my nature, but

it lay buried under my determination to move out, rifle at ready, typewriter on back, into the mist.

Yet his very naiveté and openness drew me finally to Joe. He became for me a kind of double, whom I could wonder at and admire—with amusement and a touch of disdain—as he told me about his experiences, so different from mine, on the Marianas.

His speech, like his appearance, was naive and artless—artfully artless, I realized after a while. Joe saw himself in a heroic light just as I saw myself, but from a different slant based in a different personality. Our talks soon led to a long, fond article that was featured in the old *Liberty* magazine.

A new kind of Marine hero emerged from the conquest of the Marianas.

He is not a barrel-chested, hell-for-leather assailant of pillboxes, stormer of beaches. He is a little, stooped, near-sighted man of thirty-six, whose marching gait is a compromise between a meander and a shuffle. He carries a carbine, but is a bearer primarily of peace. It is safe to say that on Saipan and Tinian islands he conquered more Japanese through love and sympathy than any one Marine disposed of with the latest automatic weapon.

Private First Class Joseph Morris Berger is from Superior, Wisconsin. He majored in ancient Greek at the University of Minnesota, found no opening to teach Plato and other classics, and so went into insurance. He came into the Marine Corps as a Marine of the line.

An insatiable curiosity about things and people caused him to start studying Japanese while still stationed in this country, and he ended up as a language interpreter for the Marines. . . .

Some Marines stormed the beaches with a grim determination not to let their buddies down. Others were moved by hatred dating from Pearl Harbor. Many were sustained by pride in their Corps. Some were buoyed by religion, some by fatalism.

But Joe Berger hit the beach with love for mankind overflowing in his heart, determined to minimize the suffering that war would bring to innocent civilians.

On the beach, I reported, Joe saw his first civilians—Japanese men past military age, women, and children—shattered and stunned by the guns of war.

They were brought down to the beach in stretchers, often by Marines and Navy corpsmen. . . . Other civilians came under their own steam, suffering from shrapnel wounds, shock, exposure, or scorched by flamethrowers. Some had wounds from attempts at suicide. Others were only frightened. They had been told that the bearded American devils would cut their throats or torture them.

I told the story of how in an improvised stockade on Saipan Joe Berger established a little kingdom of kindness, building his own corps of local Chamorro and Japanese girls to work with the doctors and corpsmen taking care of the ill, maimed, and wounded.

Some of the other translators and interpreters had laughed at Joe Berger because he insisted on learning colloquial Japanese, but now the sick, the frightened, the wounded, the dying, and the bereaved, found in him one who really understood what they said in Japanese—one to whom they could come with their problems. He worked day and night as a combination confidant, confessor, male nurse, errand boy, doctor's helper, interpreter and all-around angel of mercy.

Even as I transcribed my notes for that article, this story of a different kind of heroism shook up my sense of what was most important in the world. There was a depth in his experience. There were no longer friends and enemies, us against them, in the little kingdom Joe had created. Writing about it raised bewildering questions for me, about values and directions to be taken.

I finally could put these questions aside only by saying I was what I was. I had chosen what kind of man to be, and had better stick to it. But I could not deny that I now saw some things in a different light.

Much later, while working on this book, I decided it must have been then, under Joe's influence, that I tried to stop using the word "Jap" in my dispatches even though it was more convenient than "Japanese"; but looking over my flimsies of stories sent after that time, I see I slipped sometimes. Still, more often I either typed "Japanese" or went around the designation. Becoming steeped in Joe's experiences and being subtly exposed to his simple nobility were useful reminders about respecting everyone.

In the hot, desultory Hawaiian rest-camp months, there was time for reflection. And the dispatches written in that period seem to show a changed perspective that came from seeing the battle of Saipan through Joe Berger's huge lenses— from which the Enemy had been erased, leaving only hurt, bereaved, and bewildered people.

I typed up a story told to me by a Marine. He and another Marine were standing before a cave, getting ready to hurl grenades in. An old man popped out of the cave's mouth, looked at them, jabbered something, then hustled back in. The Marines yelled, but no one came out. The other Marine wanted to use the grenades: take no chances. The man who told me the story refused to.

Finally the old man reappeared at the mouth of the cave, lugging two stuffed suitcases. He ran in again and came out lugging still another. My Marine said, "I'll be damned," but he picked up the suitcases and carried them a quarter-mile— with the old man trotting and chattering in Japanese beside him—to a place where the suitcases and the old man could be loaded onto a truck bound for the stockade.

"So there had been no oriental mystery," I typed, "no fanaticism—merely the desire of a frightened but stubborn old man to save his belongings, goodwill on the part of the Americans, and a language barrier."

My friendship with Joe Berger had ripened to the point that I was willing to start studying Chinese with him. We went to the University of Hawaii in Honolulu twice a week, and on other evenings we studied at facing desks in the Civil Affairs quonset hut.

All this I did despite an inner voice that told me I was compromising my self-image of the sergeant, the combat correspondent who was also a kind of combat Marine. With fond disdain I observed Joe's dedication to his Chinese character cards, his total sublimation of all outside temptations to the process of mastering the language.

One night I laid aside my much smaller bundle of character cards, surreptitiously took out my notebook, and started writing a poem. I must have lost myself in it, and when I looked up Joe was not there studying opposite me. When he did not show up after a while, I decided he had left for Catlin. I went out, snapping the lock on the outside door, and caught the bus for camp.

But in fact Joe had simply dropped off to sleep over his work and fallen to the floor—and I had locked him in. By the time he managed to attract an MP, the last bus had long since left. He finally made his way to Catlin. The next morning he overslept and so could not get to the mess hall an hour early, as was his custom, to study before others arrived. He did not scold me, but I scolded myself for leaving him there, locked in. "Why didn't I look under the desk?" I demanded of the two of us.

"I'm very sorry, Levin," Joe said. "I must have been terribly tired. Perhaps I've been working too hard. I think I'll get up twenty minutes later each morning from now on."

Even the way I tell this story shows the trace of condescension in how I looked at my unworldly and unwarlike friend Joe Berger, the gentle Marine. But over and over again I was forced to realize how foolish was my pride, and how much more there was to him beneath the surface. This realization came to me strongly as I was making one more dispatch out of his experiences:

One of the strangest battles of the war was fought one night on Saipan island. It was not a battle of bullets, or shells, or bayonets, or grenades. It was a battle of ideas.

The contenders were a Marine and a Jap prisoner. At stake was a man's life—that of the Japanese.

The Marine, Private First Class Joseph Berger, of Superior, Wisconsin, was a Japanese language interpreter with the Fifth Amphibious Corps. The Jap—a 26-year-old doctor who had been helping attend wounded Japanese prisoners since his own capture by the Americans—was despondent and decided to commit hara-kiri.

The Japanese prisoner and the Marine had worked together for several days among the wounded Japanese prisoners at a Marine stockade. And the Japanese had come to like and respect the American. Therefore, when he decided to commit hara-kiri, he came to the Marine one evening with a request. He wanted the Marine to take the role of his best friend. Traditionally, when a Japanese commits hara-kiri, his best friend stands by and finishes the job by cutting off the suicide's head.

Private First Class Berger listened while the young and despondent Japanese explained that he felt guilty because he had allowed himself to be taken prisoner. He had disgraced himself and his country. Life held nothing for him.

Facing him was only imprisonment and dishonor. It was better to die and thus fulfill his vows to his country and his emperor.

"You are wrong, my friend," the Marine told him. "You are young and you have much to live for. You have not disgraced yourself or your country."

"My life is over. Of what use am I now?" the Japanese cried.

"You are of great use this very moment, taking care of your wounded countrymen and helping them survive to the day when a free Japan is born. You are learning what democracy is. When the war is over you can return to your country and help your people both as a doctor and as a man who has learned about democracy."

The young Japanese thought about it.

"I still think I must perform hara-kiri," he said reluctantly.

The American presented more arguments against suicide.

Another Marine interpreter and an Army doctor who understood Japanese came nearer to listen to the strange debate. They also urged the Japanese to choose life instead of death. It grew late in the evening. The other interpreter and the doctor went to another part of the tent and went to sleep. Still Private First Class Berger and the Japanese wrestled with the problem.

"You are not brave if you choose to die," the Marine finally charged. "You are a coward. If you choose to face life and to help your people now and after the war, you are really a brave and modern man. Japan will then be grateful for your decision."

The Japanese could not think of a good reply. His arguments grew weaker. It was now the deepest part of the night. He sat silent a moment.

"Perhaps you are right. I am all confused. All my life I thought differently about these things," he said. "I will try your way."

The Marine and the Japanese lay down to sleep. When the Marine awoke in the morning, the Japanese was hard at work, cleaning and bandaging the wounds of his captured fellow countrymen.

With some chagrin I saw that Joe Berger, my naive friend, had made himself a central actor in our war. He was the hero as healer, the champion and interpreter of our culture to the Orient. My role had to be that of the bard who sang his deeds.

The story was printed in the *Saturday Evening Post,* then still a leading journal.

Late in the year, the Chinese lessons and the whole desultory, relaxed life on Oahu suddenly ended. I was transferred to the 24th regiment of the 4th Marine Division, which was in training on the island of Maui. It would be used for either the invasion of Palau or the assault on Iwo Jima.

I did not know this and had never heard of either place. But I sensed that in its own snail-footed way, through hours and endless hours of waiting, preparing, and waiting, the vast machine of war was on the move again, and that I was being carried forward on it toward—something.

the voices of the gun, the
mud-caked, dark wound-seeping tears
that comrades dropped in the next
valley, when slaughter drew its breath.

4–Ghost Marines

Maui—our Maui—was more like Gauguin's Tahiti than like the tourist-trap and social-register Maui of today. The fine society was there even then; but we had nothing to do with it, though we shared the unbelievable natural beauty of the island. High-arcing rainbows bracketed the soft rain that fell through bright sun. The nearest town, Lahaina, consisted of only a few shacks. Lovely, untouched beaches stretched for miles. Above us were mountain slopes. The profuse consolation of nature softened the ugliness of the streets of tents in which we existed.

After standing in the sun in a long chow line, swinging our clanking and imperfectly washed out gear, we got our mess of stringy stew over a chunk of blackened toast—

and knew that "shit on a shingle" was the only apt name for it.

Becoming a regimental correspondent, far from division headquarters and lush sergeants' clubs, made for a change in status—down. I was now truly "one of the many, anonymous" I had celebrated. The forlornness of our end of the war, compared with the Europe of great cities, museums, and libraries I sometimes thought about, was coming home to me. But this had been my choice, I told myself.

In keeping with my new status, I vowed to put less prose poetry into my dispatches, to spend less time working up notes for my great war novel, and to write inspired Joe Blow stories about individual Marines. Others had died and been mutilated so as to shield the rose of freedom with their hearts— they were the heroes, I reminded myself. Write about them, Levin, not about the fucking gyrations inside your fucking head.

Then I stumbled on a Joe Blow story such as was not often granted—a whole tragic epic of heroism, compressed into platoon size.

One man did most of the telling, as he sat on his cot in his tent and I sat on a cot next to him. Others chimed in. What they told moved and thrilled me, and I knew it was what I needed to construct a story of the sort I had been sent there for. I was thorough and careful in getting the facts, checking them, and stitching them into a pattern true to reality.

Death and a platoon of Marines fought two hours over big Jim Sherwood, 21-year-old navy hospital corpsman from Milwaukie, Ore.

Death seldom met more stubborn foes.

For the comradeship of the former Willamette University pre-med student and the Marines was the kind that

makes men offer their lives for one another deliberately
and almost gladly.

It was on bloody Saipan.

A platoon of Marine pioneers of the 4th Division was
moving through a wood in skirmish line.

"We were on the left flank," said PFC B. R. Lowe Jr., 20-
year-old rifleman of Mobile, Ala. "Jim Sherwood was with
us.

"We heard shouts and machine gun fire on the right.
We ran over, and came to a small clearing across which a
Jap machine gun was firing. We went in to take that gun."

The first burst killed Pvt. Herbert E. Ericson Jr. of Grand
Rapids, Mich. He had been the group's Browning automatic rifleman. The next gust of fire caught PFC Bill Williams
of Texarkana, Tex.

"Jim Sherwood ran past me," Lowe continued. "He
would do anything for us. He was really one of us.

"He got to Bill Williams and began to give first aid. They
let go with their machine gun, and rifles. Jim was hit in
the leg. He wouldn't go back, but kept trying to help Bill.
Then he was hit again, in the chest. We saw him lean and
fall on his side."

From that point on it was their account, transmitted through
me, of how one after the other the Marines of that platoon
ran forward to try to get to Jim Sherwood and carry him back.
Their hometowns and states, as I set them down after their
names, were like a statement of the spread of America: Min-
quandale, Delaware; Newark, Glendale, and Brooklyn, New
York; Steubenville, Ohio; Mankins and Waverly, Texas;
Mishauaka, Indiana; Rock Island, Illinois; Jardine, Montana;
Tacoma, Washington; Bakersfield, California. One after another
they were hit—the platoon lieutenant, mortally wounded
carrying a stretcher toward Sherwood, and ten of the men.

They heard Japanese riflemen working around to their rear but would not stop running forward, two at a time, as if life's only purpose was to get to the wounded corpsman and bring him in. And they kept going down. Two of them did get to Sherwood and carried him behind a log, but then were themselves felled.

At last one of the men, though wounded, crawled for help and stumbled onto another unit. They had automatic weapons, and under their cover two of the men managed to get to Sherwood and carry him out of the line of fire. I concluded:

> Jim Sherwood, pharmacist's mate 3d class, died two days later, following Bill Williams whom he had tried to save and the Marines who had died trying to save Jim.
>
> The Japanese positions were finally wiped out by mortar fire and mop-up teams the next day.
>
> Bloody Saipan is in the past.
>
> The records of the killed and wounded have been compiled.
>
> The parents and loved ones of Jim Sherwood and his Marine buddies know what happened.
>
> This story is written so that others, too, may know how sometimes men will offer their lives for one another deliberately and even gladly.

Weeks later, on the transport bound for combat, I came on the bunk area where Lowe and the others were quartered. They had gotten clippings in the mail from home just before embarking. One of them showed me the story in the *Portland Oregonian,* the head spread across seven columns: HOW GALLANT JIM SHERWOOD OF OREGON DIED ON BLOODY SAIPAN.

The fellows were thrilled because the world had put its stamp on their bravery, and impressed with me as the agent. Another man had gotten a clipping from his parents in Fort Worth. The story probably ran in the hometowns of all who had died. I felt I had been united to these American heroes,

and to their widespread towns and cities. It was a total, heady
rush of reassurance.

He was a mountain youth—older than the Marines, as
many Seabees were—from one of the border states. He was
slow of speech, thoughtful, with clear values I admired. The
Seabees were attached to the pioneer battalion; he had known
the carnage of Saipan and been inspired to poetry. When we
became friends, he showed me the poem he had written.

At its center was a vision of dead Marines, appearing "in
weird pantomime . . . showing gruesome scenes before these
eyes of mine." The poet saw "many a spectre form . . . before
these eyes a frame of bone, from whose eyeless sockets light
once shown." The spectres called for "vengeance, my lad,"
as their "marching feet began to tread."

It was a poem about the terror and acknowledgment of
death. I recognized in the amateurish diction a Poe-like imagination. The man had little formal education, but he had felt
the subject, shakingly, and the poem had half-realized power:
I recognized Saipan.

I praised him and corrected some of the spelling. Afterward I brooded again about Saipan, and feelings I had not
quite brought to the surface now germinated. There is no
question that the image of ghost Marines in his poem helped
me, though the poem I now wrote was my own and very different.

When the macabre and the marvelous have met
Some sombre dusk, under a flame-tree high
Upon a pathway toward a broken Shinto shrine,
With poncho shrouded, fallen-fleshed Marines for chorus
Shrilling their lament on pipes for youth destroyed,
A Japanese girl will come all full of poetry and love
And meditate, her head bowed on her rose, still growing
Breast, where all the sacrifices and the anguish rest

Of those mad, halftrack-footed years: the voices
Of the guns, the mud-caked, dark, wound-seeping tears
That comrades dropped in the next valley, when there
Was time, when slaughter drew its breath.

That her dark eyes might play with beauty,
Their many eyes are driven fast.
That her heart like corn might open,
They have donned a shadow vast
And dreadful, till all scarlet time is ripe.
Listen. As she meditates
They in chorus stand and pipe.

The Seabee and I met again on the deck of a transport
headed for battle. I proudly showed my poem to him. He recognized the image of the ghost Marines, and by that moment's
look I knew I had hurt him badly. This was the way life treated
people like him, letting his work be exploited or stolen. I had
proved to be like others.

I could protest that his poem was imaginative doggerel
from which I had taken the idea of ghost Marines, trans-
formed it to show them piping in their circling dance, and
made it into a statement about Americans sacrificing their
lives to bring Japan to democracy. It is fair to say the same
vision of Saipan was buried in both of us, and in everyone
who had experienced that island of the dead. My poem had
many sources, but for that image—which brought it to life
and which would come to mean so much to me—I remain
grateful.

The scuttlebutt was that the next assault by the Marines
would be on Palau; then, that the 4th Division would not be
going. It would be the 1st and 3d. Two of the combat correspondents put in for transfers so they could be in on the invasion.

I didn't, partly because Palau sounded so lonely and faraway. I felt no impulse to choose it as the place where I might be sacrificed. Maybe I fancied myself, like Tolstoy's General Kutuzov, putting my ear to the ground to hear what the ground was telling me, and it was telling me to stay put until my time. I had found a home of sorts in the 24th regiment, where I could sink into sloth and not think about heroic adventures. I talked with Navaho Indians in communications, whose messages in combat would hopelessly bewilder Japanese intelligence. I even found in that communications outfit a specialist with whom I could play chess and not lose all the time.

The two correspondents who transferred were men with whom I shared a cordial dislike. One would lose his leg on Peleliu island in the Palau group. That news made me uneasy—as if I had let him go in my place.

We waited.

There were swimming tests for each battalion. In boot camp we all had to swim one-hundred yards, and I just made it. This time we only had to do seventy-five yards—and I just made it.

I became friends with a young American couple—he was Anglo and she was Chinese-American. They lived far away from everything, surrounded by the soft, dancing Hawaiian hills, which I painted, and by pineapple plantations. I would talk with Sam and Marion about philosophy and Buddhism and all kinds of other topics as if such things were real, though I knew they could not be in my present life.

How come Sam was a civilian? Was he a conscientious objector, or a 4F? I never bothered to ask. If I saw my situation at all, the image I saw was of a vast hand in whose palm I was being carried into the future.

I got a package, which had traveled for months to reach this Hawaiian base, from my father in Cleveland. It was filled with cans of Hawaiian pineapple.

I thought about Joe Berger, who was back on Oahu with the translators. I missed our evenings in the quonset hut, each shuffling through flash cards with Chinese characters on one side and English equivalents on the other; and I missed the trueing of values that Joe's own character provided.

I lay on an absolutely empty, immaculate stretch of beach beyond Lahaina. Time rolled by, not even noticed. Life seemed to float, suspended.

Soon after New Year's Day 1945, the waiting ended.

I had been getting ready for Iwo Jima long before I knew there was an Iwo Jima.

I had come in on D plus 9 on Saipan. By the morning of D plus 2 on Tinian, when I landed, there was no more resistance on or near the beach. You've got to go in early, I coached myself.

The regiment drew additional gear on Tuesday. The transports lay in the harbor at Wailuku. We marched to the flagpole on Thursday, then piled into six-by-sixes. Truck after truck, knee to knee, facing each other, we jolted down the precipitous, sea-girdled roads.

The many trucks churned up dust, and all our faces became masked with it. We tried to peer out past the canvas flaps. It seemed to me that heretofore hidden beauties that had surrounded our lives were suddenly emerging from all sides, mocking us. The rainbow, which we had come to expect, lifted its great arch over the mountains, marking our departure as it had marked our arrival. We looked with the longing that one feels for parting friends at the leaning palms, the wayside hibiscus and poinciana that burned brightly, the oleanders whose odor seemed to reach after us. I saw in every Marine's face the same rending regret they must have seen in mine, for something we could not define that would now be lost to us. It was a very strange ride, a very silent one.

The truck convoy avoided the town, taking another road to the docks. There the regiment unloaded from the trucks.

At a creeping shuffle each unit single-filed up the gangways, and up the finality of the gangways into the ships.

The guns and other heavy equipment had been loaded earlier. The loading had been going on for weeks. The men took two days to load. The following day we sailed. The transports headed toward Pearl Harbor, to meet up there with the rest of the convoy.

We must have had liberty for some days, before the convoy set out from Pearl. I went to the base for a good meal in the sergeants' club and to see Joe Berger. He was not going on this invasion. In the intelligence hut on the base I found a briefing brochure lying around that named the Bonin or Volcano Islands as one possible target.

What the higher echelons knew did not filter down, and I didn't care. What I did care about was being in this coming battle, wherever it was, from the start, and sending a series of dispatches that would startle the world. My Hermes typewriter was ready; we had been issued carbines before the Tinian landing, to replace the heavier M-1s, and mine was clean. I regretted losing the M-1. It was far more romantic.

I resolved to begin writing my dispatches on the transport while we crossed the Pacific, so that the approach to battle and then the battle itself, seen through one pair of eyes, would be documented. I also planned to write a cycle of poems representing every stage of the experience.

Being assigned to the pioneer battalion was a bad disappointment. It would be going in late, for such units always went in after the infantry waves had secured the beach. That was not good enough. My next dispatch had to be sent under fire from the beachhead.

I buckled on all my resolutions, like a samurai buckling on armor. I had no idea what it was that I was looking forward to—and didn't want to know. I had managed to forget, or put out of mind, the worst of the emotions of Saipan. Having come in late, and having been on the periphery of the

battle's terror and revulsion, made this loss of memory possible. Writing the island of the dead into a poem helped me
deal with the experience. Believing in the war—whatever
that now meant, at this great distance—also helped. Some
instinct told me, as I think it tells everyone, it was better that
way.

Beginning the long voyage
For many the longest
The last night prophetic
The ships moored together
Like giant sea-huddled sisters
Music streaming from one
Borne across several decks.
High on the bridge of ours,
Chained in emotion, we watch
The bright movie pulsing
On the deck of the next.

5—Destination Iwo

It was the night before the departure of the troop transports for combat. Our transport lay alongside the others at anchor in Pearl. The battle fleet had gone on ahead and was already pounding Iwo, but we did not know this. The transports on their long slow voyage would be shielded by zigzagging destroyers and destroyer escorts.

Most of the Marines sat on deck late that evening. I was in the group that had climbed to the bridge. Leaning on the rail we could look across to the deck of the next transport, where a movie was showing on a screen. It may have been Bing Crosby in *White Christmas,* or something else full of stateside quarrels, joys, and complexities.

There on the bridge as I watched the movie, the first poem

came to me of what I was determined would be a series memorializing this voyage and the battle to follow. I wrote its title: "The Departure." The last stanza expressed what not only I but so many must have felt, under the excitement and dazed bravado, in those opening moments of what would be our life's critical experience.

> High the waste moon riding
> Waste fields of heaven
> A ship's light broken
> To crazed flashing splinters
> Like our lives, like our futures,
> On the mysterious waters.

It was not a particularly warm Hawaiian night. The slight chill increased the sense of wonder and strangeness, the alertness toward unimagined vistas. Long after, I would write about that night as the herald of a great modern epic of nobility and pathos "that one day will be sung when the world is colder and the stars have shifted. . . ." So much has happened since to shake all convictions. How uplifted I felt that night, how certain that we were setting out on an epic as worthy of song as any in the world's history.

Then at dawn, leaning eagerly on the rail, "very early morning: the fleet leaves Pearl Harbor," I wrote under the title of the next poem in the cycle. The excitement, strangeness, and heroic glamour (drowning out any sense of the real nature of the business we were bent upon) filled and seemed to swell me, as if I were part of the huge ship itself. For the title I invoked those "Strange Stars and Skies" we were sailing toward.

> Parade, strange stars and skies.
> Flank and wheel, company mass.
>   Fix your shining bayonets, stand
>   like silver and blue lions,
>   eternal feet spread firmly.

> We will sail by, and away
>   to our future.

I was already planning, partly consciously, my war novel.

All religious faiths leave their mark, and the defective religion of communism had left its mark on me. I still had to pay
an abandoned idealism its due. And so the proletarian hero
I had once conjured up (like so many growing up in that age
the war had terminated) remained as an image waiting to
become part of my Marine hero, the Polish American youth
Glenn Manson.

Another part of him was of course myself—ten years
younger. But a big part of him, too, was a straight-out, repor-
torial, affectionate depiction of the youths I—ten years and
more older than they—had come to know in boot camp, and
to know again as I took part in their vast experiences.

These were the same youths from society's lower rungs I
had once idealized; but now they were real. They were the
realest thing in my present life. They enclosed and filled it.
I saw them, limned against the sky.

EN ROUTE TO ——— (Delayed)—A soft evening. The
transport rocking forward rhythmically. Mauve clouds ringing the horizon suffused with slowly fading rose.

On the hatch cover, perched on boxes and camp stools,
were four Marines in dungarees. They fingered their bat-
tered instruments—a sax, a clarinet, drums, a bass horn.
Massed around them, standing, sitting on the deck or on
piles of rope, astride machinery, or braced against the rail,
were their buddies of the Marine infantry.

The ship's loudspeaker had brought the radio news:
"Iwo Jima hit by B-29s . . . Red Army advances . . . New
landings on Luzon. . . ." Now they waited patiently for the
evening concert.

The clarinet suddenly tootled, and the little band swung
into Beer Barrel Polka.

A British army colonel, with the troops as an observer, stood on the deck above in his highland kilts, beaming on the assemblage.

"He'll freeze his balls off," one of the Marines observed.

Two men bumped together as they squirmed toward a better spot. They glared, then recognized one another as hometown buddies.

"Hey, you old fucker!" the first man shouted. "How long you been out here?"

"Eighteen months. Three campaigns. I'll get stateside after this."

"Hell, you'll be here for the China coast," the other replied calmly.

They turned to listen to the music.

"Put on your Easter bonnet . . ."

Many sang or hummed.

The general came out and stood at the rail, looking down.

"Who kin play the gee-tar?" one of the musicians yelled.

A lanky North Carolina boy pushed through the massed Marines and jumped up on the hatch. They gave him the idle guitar. He strummed.

"Hotdog. He's good."

"I'll be down to get you in a taxi, honey . . ." The guitar strummed, clarinet tootled, sax moaned and lilted.

Darkness had descended, like a gentle curtain, veiling the future. The rose had faded, the mauve clouds had sunk. The constellation of Orion unfolded. A large planet burned.

When the music ended, the men broke into restless groups. Some stood shooting the breeze on deck. Others filed down the steep iron stairs into the holds. On the walls of their compartments, terrain maps had been put up. This was The Word. They were to assault ————.

The lanky North Carolina boy's name I filled in later, on the original copy that was sent stateside to his hometown paper (with "fuck" deleted) after the landing. IWO JIMA would be filled in on the dateline, and at the end of the story, in Washington—also after the landing. We were still a week away, then, from Iwo.

I never learned if that young gee-tarist survived the battle. The passing along of The Word I would describe, with the allowances given to fiction, in my novel.

"This is Dai Shima island," Joe DiNardi went on. He stood beside the map and pointed with a pencil.

"It's only about four hundred miles from Japan."

"Cozy-like," said Bill Obradovich.

"You see how it looks, like a shoe, or more like a slipper, pointing northeast. This is Orange Beach. This is Purple Beach. This is Blue Beach."

"No Purple Heart Beach?" Bill Combes asked.

"No."

"Every fucking beach on that fucking Enibaru was Purple Heart Beach," Combes explained around him. "Don't let them names snow you."

"We don't know much about Dai Shima," DiNardi went on.

"Oh that's all right," Chicken put in, "we'll find out."

"Knock it off," Lewicki said.

On the transport was a platoon that carried demolition satchels and flamethrowers. It was named "the assault platoon" and was part of the second battalion of the 24th regiment, which was mine.

I started hanging around their bunks and made friends with the men of the assault platoon. Combat correspondents had a way of being adopted as good luck charms of a sort, anyway. Their platoon leader, a second lieutenant, was a fine-featured quiet young man, Joe LoPrete (who became DiNardi in my novel).

Their platoon sergeant, Frank Krywicki, was a straightforward, able, modest, determined man, with whom I soon felt there could be lasting friendship. Frank did his duty without dreaming it was idealism—as I did. My portrait of "Lewicki" in my novel was a slightly idealized portrait of the real man.

I would follow him, my gallant platoon sergeant, into the landing boat, out of it onto that terrible beach, into that first night's foxhole, and later, once, as far as my nerves and very modest courage would allow me, into the savage sulphur-pitted wilderness of my dispatches.

I decided I would land not with the pioneers—late on D-day, or that evening, or even the next morning—but with the assault platoon. I went to see the major who commanded the battalion, and cleared it. Then I was thrilled and happy, and vaguely aware I was terrified.

My acceptance into the brotherhood of the assault platoon was sealed when I became part of the breakout detail. We brought food from deep in the ship to feed the multitude.

We filed into the moist cold of the refrigeration room, tugged out heavy crates of potatoes, heaved them onto our shoulders, and staggered out. Four men at the top of the steep iron ladder held one end of a rope, and someone at the foot of the ladder knotted the other end and passed the loop around one of the crates. We strained at the rope, blistering our hands, getting the crate on a board laid over the stairs, on which it was dragged up. We kept filing back and forth, swaying under more crates of potatoes, till the next day's supply of sixteen crates had been hauled up and carried away to the galley.

Then came oranges—ten crates—an orange apiece for morning chow except for the last couple of hundred men in line. The crates were stacked ceiling high, teetering with the roll of the ship.

We took a five-minute break before starting to tug at these crates. Each man tore the skin from one or two oranges and sank his teeth into the fiercely cold, tangy fruit. Like lotus-eaters in the depths of the sea, we crammed the searing cold chunks of fruit into our mouths. We stuck oranges in our dungaree pockets, to eat later. These were legitimate spoils.

Returning to work, we dragged the orange crates out to the foot of the ladder, to be pulled up by hand. As the last of them slid up the ramp, one of us unbolted the hatch to the meat room. Lungs contracting with the drier, fiercer cold, we plunged in to lift carcasses wrapped in blood-smeared oilskin paper. The biggest men lurched, grunting, up the ladder, each bearing a great hunk of bloody meat.

We worked for two hours after every morning chow, and for two or three hours after evening chow. If a man doped off one night, he made up for it by carrying more than his share the next time. I had never been more alive, more united with others, more happy—yes, happy—to be giving of myself with unstinting, exhausting effort.

A letter, typed but signed in a scrawl "Sgt Dan Levin," must have cleared the censoring officer on the transport and been sent off with the rest of the mail on a destroyer.

Kitty, my flamethrowers (with whom I will go in, then join my pioneers the night of D day or the next morning) are the rowdy, loud, roistering, warmhearted, impulsive, loyal, jealous, lovable, fierce, proud, scrappy, brawling, ragamuffin bad boy Marines—they stand out among the rest of the 4th division because they are louder, swagger more, are more kiddish, know how, get around, fuckoff, pitch in and help, get and give, grab, quarrel, bellyache, beat their

gums, are clannish, proud of being Marines, curse the
Corps, are everything human without stint. I like them
and am already sentimentally attached to them, and I
believe they really like me.

The inner circle includes Ben Greenberg, Bill Tolarovich,
Walt Burkowski, Steve Veeder, Harmon, and one or two
others. Greenberg is the natural leader and the nucleus—
it may be that the gang is basically good and warm because
its leader is a Jew (precluding anti-Semitism and forcing,
tacitly, acceptance of ideas of democracy and tolerance).
He is loud, expressive, boisterous, headstrong, beautifully
built, sexually attractive, frank. He wants to go back to his
girl friend back [home]. He has "scored" on many girls (illus-
trated by the appropriate motions—one hand striking the
bicep of the other, which moves forward like an engine pis-
ton). He dreams of another girl, with whom he went long
ago but now she comes back in the dream and he chooses
her after a struggle with himself (all this told loudly and
naively and frankly and seriously). He dreams of being back
in Dorchester (Boston) where he was the Terror of Elling-
ton Street. That Ganiff Greenie. He has no illusions. He has
been fucked again and again by the Corps. But a fierce
pride in the Corps. Bill Tolarovich is the son of a Pennsylvania coal miner, slick and ingratiating, and serious, and
humorous, and knowing that his life depends on himself—
I have not yet explored him as much. A handsome blond
boy, with a sense for the subtly mock-heroic (his shoes cut
out until they are some kind of eerie sandal, permitting
"ventilation")—coming from him not a straight statement
but one juicy with sly mock-heroism. Manned a machine
gun in the Marshalls, piling up slew of Japs trying for break-
through. His buddy (wounded, and having fired the gun
only briefly) got Navy Cross, he got nothing. His favorite
expressions the usual fuck and shit and—my goodness.
Harmon is from Kentucky, talks in a high, premeditated

and artistically tough nasal twang which is pure Churchill
Downs, Brooklyn. His reputation rests on knowing every
horse that ever won Kentucky Derby and the year. In reality, the kid knows one or two, is at least five years off on
those, doesn't know Equipoise, but will come back with a
snappy and confident answer without hesitation. This
snows some, others haven't the heart to say anything. "Who
won in 1927, Harmon?" "Gallant Fox." "See," says Greenberg, turning to me. "A fucking sharpie. Does he know his
Derby! Does he know his horses! I'm whipped! That's all.
I'm whipped." Now even I know that this is at least 10 years
off, but who am I. Harmon stands with his blue eyes aggres-
sive and impudent and laughing. Oh, one I shouldn't forget is Frenchy Bellemere who speaks a canuck French and
whose English is often so mumbled that it is impossible to
understand. Warm-hearted, rough and ready, sweet with
a curious sweetness of the strange boy with an enclosed,
different background and who thinks slantwise in relation
to the others. On the fringe is Moriarty, who has studied
psychoanalysis, is refined and sensitive, and clean and
good. His jaw and neck still bear the grownover scar of a
bullet wound that went through the jaw while he was getting a wounded man to cover under fire on Saipan. Greenberg went out then and brought Moriarty in.

I could go on a while. They are dear to me.

A few days bloodshot and terrible will climax and end
all. All of this great and fearful wrenching of thousands
upon thousands from all they know and love will be resolved
in a couple of sunrises and sunsets and ghastly nights.
Those of us who live will never return to what we were.
Always our beings will come back to the dead center of
this February, always.

Influenced by Joe Berger's experiences, I had begun to
avoid using "Jap" for "Japanese" in my dispatches. Reading

over this letter again, I see I typed "slew of Japs"—and these were not Bill Tolarovich's words but mine. This means that even en route to Iwo I was struggling with that problem of the word to use. We are creatures of our environment as well as conviction.

The usage was not racist, though it might be construed that way. It was the natural, and American, desire to do and say things more easily and informally. I heard no crap about the "yellow peril" among our young Marines. The mass suicides on Saipan—both the suicide banzais and the leaps off the cliffs at Marpi Point—had made many of our fellows believe they were facing a mysterious nation of fanatics; that's something else. I knew even then, from dispatches, that a Nisei regiment was bleeding and winning gratitude on the Italian front. Out here, it was "Jap."

A reasonably honest compromise was the one I used in story no. 9: I reported the Marines saying "Japs" and added, later, my own way of saying it—"Japanese troops." The story was slugged: 75,000 IS A CROWD.

EN ROUTE TO ———— (Delayed)—Two Marines were staring out over the water, in the direction of ————.

One said, "There'll be 60,000 Marines hitting that island."

"Yeah," the other added, "and there's supposed to be 15,000 Japs on it ain't there?"

"That's right. And it's only 10 square miles."

The second Marine sighed.

"Somebody's gonna have to get off," he said.

After our last briefing the island could be named, so I added to the copy:

As it turns out, there were 30,000 Japanese troops, not 15,000, on Iwo Jima, and the island was 8, not 10, square miles.

A conversation with a charter member of the assault platoon:

ABOARD A TRANSPORT, EN ROUTE TO ———— (Delayed)—
"We'll take it. So we'll take it, that's all," Ben said. "You know why?"

"No."

"Because we got to take it. We got to, that's all."

"How come?"

"Because we're the Marines, that's how come. Because everything we hit we take. Because we took Guadal, we took Tarawa, we took Saipan, we took Guam. Every damn island they send us to take, we took."

We stared out into the dark night. The water foamed away from the side of the transport, cutting ahead relentlessly toward the island.

"No matter what happens, no matter what they do to stop us, no matter how many we lose, the rest of us are going to get ashore. You ask me how come I know? I know the men we got, I know what they can do. I got confidence in them. And you know what?"

"What?"

"Every other Marine feels like I do," Ben said. "They know we got to take it. So I know one thing. We'll take that ————."

Our dispatches were still not naming Iwo Jima. In two or three days they would.

After chow and breakout detail were long over I would lie on the hatch covers in the Pacific evening, looking up at the myriads of universes gazing down so patiently, calmly, and uncaringly while the transport rocked rhythmically. After a while sleep would come, and I might sleep away part of the night before going down to my bunk.

One night, lying there, the welded deck groaning and

rocking beneath me, I looked up for a long time at the mast the sailors called the Charlie Noble. It swayed like a pendulum between me and that field of stars. Looking past it, I tried to fix on one of the stars. Finally I rolled onto my side, got out the pencil from my breast dungaree pocket and the notebook from the side pocket, and wrote what I imagined that "seraphim-wise" star felt as its light cleaved down to see the anguish and desolation of us humans.

> What a dismay would darken its lovely face—
> Its calm would crack—it would totter—shrivel—
> Parabola headlong howling and crying.
> Like a candelabra torn from the roof of the temple, from
>   perennial existence,
> Fall, star, shrieking and burning
> From high, happy, ceaseless perfection!

I dated the poem: February 16. I knew we were approaching the island.

I was puzzled, too. Here I was in the midst of an adventure I knew would be life's high-water mark, believing in the war's justness, full of heroic fustian about throwing myself forward on liberty's altar; but when I relaxed, in the change of guard from evening to night, this dark finding was what I came up with.

By the time of my next dispatch to Marine Corps headquarters, the shadow of that terrible island had fallen on all of us. I believe I captured the atmosphere of those last days and their premonitions. The story had an impact; it was distributed by the Associated Press.

> ABOUT ONE HUNDRED MILES OUT OF IWO JIMA—(Delayed)—
> "The fellows don't argue or snarl at each other hardly at all today. They're gentler. When one guy steps on another guy's foot, he doesn't get cursed nearly as much."

"You ask why? Because every fellow is thinking. Thinking that somebody ain't coming back. And every fellow is thinking maybe he's going to be the one that ain't coming back."

Protestant services are piped, on hatch two, to be followed by Catholic services. Jewish services, conducted by a strapping, gray-haired master technical sergeant, had been held Friday in the chief petty officers' mess.

"Me, I always say—I'm coming back. I got to come back. Roi, Namur, Saipan, Tinian, now this Iwo Jima. They can't touch me. I got to come back."

It is bright sunlight, but only moderately warm. The sun is on our left, on its way down. The ship races North.

For the first time in this war the Marines will attack north of the Tropic of Cancer.

The noon radio had told of Japanese broadcasts claiming repulse of a landing attempt on Iwo Jima—a landing which we know we are to take part in tomorrow morning.

It had told of our continued bombardment of the island from the sea and air, and of violent anti-aircraft fire. The Japanese radio claimed shore batteries had smashed one of our ships of war.

Until that broadcast—the unmistakable overtones of a great engagement in its first phase—many had hoped in their hearts that it would be easy after all. Now all know it will be hard—the Marine Way.

Services begin on the hatch.

". . . in the face of tomorrow's uncertainties . . ."

It has grown perceptibly colder. Clouds in sombre layers darken away the sun.

". . . He leadeth me beside the still waters . . ."

Four American fighter planes whirr over, headed for their parent carrier after a reconnoitering flight.

". . . I am the resurrection and the way . . ."

After the Protestant services there is communion. A

brigadier general and a private first class kneel side by side.

Catholic services . . . The regimental chaplain in his white robe . . . The suppliants kneeling on the welded deck.

The sea is rougher, the wind chill.

The men stand waiting to use the washrooms, before chow. They are restless. Some are absorbed in thought.

A lieutenant inspects a rifle platoon. The men flick dust off their M-1's and BAR's as they wait their turn.

The great Sunday evening meal is piped—the meal for which Marine "breakout" crews and Marine and Navy cooks and messmen hauled and froze and sweated, in refrigerators and holds deep in the belly of the transport.

The only unusual thing about the noon meal had been the salt tablets given each man—against tomorrow's excessive running and sweating and against possible shock from wounds.

But here, at last, are the great turkeys (ship "scuttlebutt" for days before), warm rolls, ice cream and pie, and other rich food to make the men full and strong for tomorrow.

The threat of rain grows.

The chill increases.

Darkness creeps forward, sadly and quickly on cloud-feet.

The men enjoy their meal, even after the almost endless chowline leading down to the mess where they eat standing. The food has to take the place of everything good and joyful—of sweetheart, wife, child, mother, friends, home beside the radio, dawns and evenings without terror. . . .

The main thing is not that it has grown suddenly dark and cold, but that it has grown suddenly lonely.

Behind lies everything.

Ahead only the Volcanoes—D day in the shadow of the Japanese mainland.

Now I commit myself to the depth and the wave
To the spirit of unfolding the things that must
unfold and of folding the things to be folded
Spirit that balances things as they rise from
the night out of life into life and retire
to the night into life out of life

6–Days of Wrath

There is no sound like heavy naval gunfire in the distance, in the night. It conjures up a deep-voiced dramatic doom, something so profound and impersonal and assured that it is more than ominous, it is both awe-filled and prophetic.

It was a prophetic night. I knew that eternal possibilities were afloat, that the reports of those naval guns rolling and echoing off the steel sides of the ship, coming to us in the holds in heavy, regular pounding muffled undertones, were describing something scrolled in the book of fate and impenetrable.

The poem written that night may be the closest I could ever come to expressing what ultimates I believe in, my version of the larger-than-myself or -ourselves.

I called it "Before Combat" and dated it "the night of February 18–19." At its end, I committed

My hands, and my feet, my eyes, my head,
    my brains, my manhood, myself—
To the depth, the wave, and the spirit of things
    that fold and unfold
In the calm of the night, in the grip and the
    roll of the sea.

I am usually reticent, as many Americans are, about these things. They are the substratum, the chthonic holy place where the spirits circle forever, and I do not believe in invoking them except rarely. Generally all is silent in that great realm, except when a few words momentarily lift the veil, showing for that moment the enigmatic seal of the mystery.

After the first waves had set out, I wandered around the ship, waiting for the assault platoon's turn. Several times I must have gone to the "head" to urinate. Scuttlebutt was passed along—that casualties in the first wave were "moderate." What did "moderate" mean? After a while I saw, without wanting to see, wounded men being hauled aboard in rope nets.

Hours passed, and I kept seeing the landing craft going in. Unlike my indelible first imprint of Saipan, there remains no clear visual first memory of Iwo Jima—except possibly one of a clublike hulk, mostly veiled in smoke. The day was dark. The landing craft kept disappearing behind the smoke banks. I must have been blocking out everything else. I had no curiosity. I would know soon enough.

Finally I wandered down the steel ladder and into the assault platoon's area. The men were rolling on their leggings and getting their gear and flamethrowers and demolition satchels ready. I had a single pack, with my typewriter in it. I think I stuffed a pair of socks into my dungaree pocket.

After a time, as if by unspoken agreement (though either LoPrete or Frank Krywicki must have given the word, which I did not hear), all began to file to the steel ladder, and I followed the men ahead of me up on deck and to the rail.

The poem written the night before had marked the last preparation for the ritual descent into death's kingdom. The first physical stage of the descent itself was something I had foreseen but whose reality I could not have imagined. In fact, from this point, about two o'clock in the afternoon in the world we were leaving behind, events moved in a dazed montage of action, fear, and determination.

I went backward down the rope ladder into the landing craft, my typewriter in its pack swinging wildly and pulling at me. I missed the last rung and dropped on my heels in the landing craft, but was caught by one of the other men. We settled down in it, one against the other.

The water was sad and rough, the sky leaden.

Often I have struggled trying to establish a true chronology for those next hours, to wrench them out of their surreality so I could explain them coherently to others and to myself. I know we circled, and sat dead in the water, and again circled for a long time, with the other landing craft of our wave; that much, and the anxiety of the wait, I know for sure. Then the craft straightened out and went faster, straight, with resolve, and I saw at last, in a quick look, that we had started toward the flashing pall of smoke.

The trip in was a thing of profound resignation, congealed thought, emotion searing and diffuse. I sat facing backward in the boat, trying to guess what I could from the changing degrees of wonder and dismay and consternation that in succession shaded the Navy coxswain's face. Only a few times did I glance up from my helmet at Frank Krywicki, who was standing upright as a platoon sergeant should. Frank's face was impassive, while the rest of us crouched, sometimes glancing up. (Much later he would tell me he had watched a craft next to us get blown out of the water, but said nothing so as not to unsettle us.)

In one instant I heard an abrupt violent howl and the boat lifted, then rammed forward grating and stopped with a shock. We were all hurled off our feet. Over to the side some yards away, I saw—from my eye-corner—a clump of black tossed far into the air. I did not consciously think—there was no time, nor could I believe—That's a man's body! I forgot it instantly. The ramp had ripped down. A smell I imagined— but I smelled it!—of roasted and burning flesh swept into my nostrils. I leaped ashore on a new and fearful world.

That first moment's awful sight was one that mortals should not be forced to see—or else that all, without exception, should be forced to see. Figures of men, and half-figures of men, lay about in the dark, smoky sand. My eyes and mind slid away from them, but not without the instant realization that the strange quickness by which all men recognize each other's existence had gone out of these figures. Theirs was no longer a human but a waxen essence.

I must have run hard, through the ankle-deep water and then the heavy black sand; then fell forward into it, in a depression scooped out by some shell. I burrowed my body into the sand but kept glaring around, still startled and unbelieving.

A fierce unnatural light imbued the island and the sky and burned each moment into organic memory. It seemed to me as if my whole life had been an effort to veil this moment and obscure this inevitable scene, and that at last the veil had been torn aside and the final nightmare vision of life revealed.

Events had become released from any definite order. I know (because I figured it out later) my glasses were blown off my face by the shock as the craft struck the shore violently; later I realized I did not need them. I know I sat at the water's edge a dazed moment, staring at the big dark stain on my dungarees where I had wet myself.

I lay there in the sand, wanting not to fear, terribly, that the next howling sound would be the one. Each time I heard an explosion I knew I was all right until the next one. Kid Harmon and Greenberg must have been beside me . . . maybe Frenchy Bellemere . . . Gene Jones the combat photographer must have joined us.

Once I turned my head to look over my shoulder and saw rising in the ocean behind our clublike island, so close I could throw a stone at it, another even more sinister island. It was a cone, perfect and weird and magical—an antarctic mirage out of Poe's ghostly story of Gordon Pym. There it was, peering down as I peered up at it from the ashen sand—sharp-etched in sudden renewed sunlight, as if the sun itself had come back mockingly from the dead to reveal it. (It was probably Mount Suribachi, seen over my shoulder to the south.)

And when I turned my head away, there beside me—but surely this came later!—lay a Marine with a beautiful face and shoulders and all below the shoulders a viscous, red-shot, and dragging mess of rag.

And sometime also I heard someone speaking to me as I burrowed there. "Could any of you help us carry two boys down? There's only two of us, and he's heavy."

I was terrified to stand upright. Every instinct was to stay curled and pressed flat into the sand. But I saw that by some mute counter-instinct I had gotten up and was motioning to Gene Jones, and he was getting up and, naked targets on that dark frightening beach, we were walking toward the man on the stretcher and bending and picking the stretcher up. Both he and I were obeying some kind of inner law, I think, that training and bonding had strengthened—just enough.

We and the two corpsmen carried the stretcher to the water's edge. The man had a thigh wound. He kept murmuring something, and I made out it was that his brother had been a Navy corpsman, killed in Italy. He was trying to let us know he was grateful.

We put the stretcher down at the water's edge, and ran back and fell into the sand again.

We lay listening to the mortar sounds, sphincters tightened.

And still no word that we could get off that beach.

Where can I place another image imprinted forever: an embrace, of sorts, between a Marine and a Japanese? Each had been torn away except for the head and some entrails— the Japanese boy by our shelling, the American boy later by Japanese shell or mortar fire. The two helmeted heads lay facing each other, with such pained and soulful expressions on the two faces that I could hardly bear to look. Their entrails curled around and their ends met, twining about each other.

I don't know whether I came upon them that first hour on the beach, or early on D-day plus 1 when I returned there. I was so shocked that I made a drawing in my notebook of that embrace.

At last word came from LoPrete, carried by Krywicki running from one group of three or four men of the platoon to the next, that we were to get off the beach now. We were frantic to comply, before the mortars could search us out lying there.

We ran stumbling over the hurdles of broken figures, one of them on hands and knees, stopped in his Marine forward rush with huge concave dent in his unhelmeted head, and over headless trunks and over legs and all the other grotesque and frozen postures of high-velocity death. We churned painfully through the sand, up an incline. I carried a demo satchel for Frenchy part of the way so he could carry the flamethrower; after we stopped for breath and started our

panting uphill run again, I lugged one of the other flamethrowers, spelling someone (maybe Harmon). On the third spurt
we reached a matted growth of shrubs and knew we were
off the beach.

There in the sand amid the tangled growth we started
digging ragged foxholes. As I dug I suddenly unearthed a
huge, torn, venomously bright-colored bird that must have
been destroyed by our fire. In a spasm of unreasoned disgust
I hurled it away.

The foxhole I helped dig was big enough for three—me
and Frenchy, I think, and Gene—to curl up tight against one
another. We did not know where we were, though we wanted
to believe the remains of those earlier waves were ahead of
us. But there was no way of knowing. Because of this we did
not try to communicate with other units. We stayed put, talking in whispers and waiting while evening changed to night.
We scooped out sand and urinated in the foxhole. We fell into
a frightened, emotionally spent sleep, but I started to snore.
That scared Gene even more, so he shook me awake. We lay
there all night, scrunched together, fitfully sleeping, while
from the rugged ground beyond the airport the Japanese
poured artillery fire over our heads onto the beach. It deci-
mated the pioneer battalion I was first assigned to and had
promised to rejoin. It never occurred to me to go back to that
terrible beach, once we had managed to quit it.

Within that first hour and a half on the beach, still pressed
into the black sand with the dead all around, I had also scratched
down notes and even managed to pull the Hermes out of its
pack and typed up at least a draft of the following story. This
is as hard as anything for me to believe today, but the time
given in the story is right—five o'clock on the afternoon of D-
day—and there is immediacy in the details. I must have finished it the next morning, in that foxhole.

IWO JIMA, VOLCANO ISLANDS, BONIN GROUP—(Delayed)—A shell hit about 100 yards on the left, and a man was hurled into the air. We waited, down in a shellhole about 20 feet from the water's edge, cursing and asking why we didn't get the word to move in off the goddam beach. Five o'clock D-day.

Suddenly we saw two men of the assault platoon walk across the terrible beach, dragging between them something that writhed and shook and was like jelly.

"What is it? Who is it?"

"It's little ———," Ben said sadly, digging his face deeper into the ground. "Cracked up."

They dragged him into a shell hole and laid him down and called for the corpsmen.

"A good man, too," said Ben. "A damn good little man. Good on the Marshalls, Saipan, Tinian. How much can one man take? Too much is too much."

There were six hundred of our dead on Blue, Yellow, Red, Green, and Purple beaches by D-day night. After that, the rate would be about a hundred KIA a day.

On the morning of D plus 1 I went back down to the beach to get that story onto one of the craft taking wounded back to the ships. Shelling began, and they were hitting close. Another of the combat correspondents, Bill Dvorak, who had worked on a Cleveland paper, was going down at the same time, and we fell to the sand next to each other.

Suddenly I was sure I was doomed that morning. I held out my copy to him. "In case I don't make it—" I breathed. With an abrupt gesture of utter outrage and loathing, he panted, "Take your goddam copy down yourself."

I did finally get it down myself, to a Navy coxswain taking wounded out to the hospital ship in an LCVP.

It was probably this story that was wired from the ship

and put on the radio. My wife was working in Washington, doing maps for the Joint Chiefs of Staff. The other women came to her, led her to the lounge, sat her down, and told her that her husband's dispatch had just been read on the radio. That meant I had been alive the previous day. She sat there weeping.

Later that day I watched a Marine dying on the beach. Two corpsmen stood over him, one on each side, with plasma bottles uptilted. His collapsed veins were refusing to take the plasma. Though his body was still writhing, his face was already turning the color of earth. I stood behind the corpsmen, helpless to do anything but take notes for what could not become a dispatch. It had to be a poem.

I visualized the corpsmen as benedictory angels, and his soul, struggling to escape from the writhing agony of the body, as a child unwilling to leave the old doorway of its home "even when the home is shattered, the door fallen." I addressed that soul:

> Pick up your seabag, soul,
>> the ocean of light is endless
>>> many white worlds beckon.
>> Say adieu and go. Look,
>>> hundreds upon hundreds
>>>> on the beaches all around you
>>>>> quitting their shattered homes
>>>>>> are bravely setting forth.

The indenting of the lines throughout the poem was meant to suggest the wings of the benedictory angels.

Some of the feeling in it, as well as in some of my reportage, would go into my war novels. Some material would be transferred into the fictions nearly intact. I took scribbled notes and typed on the beach, in a giant foxhole dug later on high ground by order of the division PRO (with whom I managed to get along, barely), and during stops on my meanderings between the beach and the assault platoon's foxholes.

Throughout D-day plus 1 mortar shells from the ground to the north kept coming in sporadically. I would guess where the next one might go, and zigzag. The dead still lay unburied. My next dispatch merged this D plus 1 setting with experiences still resonating in me from D-day.

IWO JIMA, VOLCANO ISLANDS—(Delayed)—Yesterday this beach was full of death and the frantic effort of men to drive forward from the beach and stay alive. Today it is a place of confusion and terror, for the men on it today must stay there and bring in the ammo and load it, and take care of the wounded. They can only stay, and huddle, and wait, and take it.

The beach is a mortar and artillery beach. It climbs up terraces, bare and open to the raking fire from Suribachi volcano and the guns of the airfield and the guns of the rugged ground on the right. It is a beach of men sprawled waxen and limp as dolls, and of the mangled remains of men whom shellfire tore out of their original human form. It is a beach on which each wave crouched in great grim shellholes, the living among the dead, cursing and waiting to move out, to get off the terrible beach to higher ground.

"The hell with this," said one Marine veteran of three previous campaigns. "I should of stayed home."

A beautiful blond boy sprawls half covered by a poncho. The poncho covers a body crushed and blown out of all human resemblance. The face is composed and still.

The Japanese artillery and mortar strength has gone beyond our anticipations. Therefore it is a brutal beach, where the law of averages calls the shots and the Marine just crouches and curses or prays.

A little doctor, already a hero at Saipan, stands erect and calls for volunteers to carry the wounded on stretchers.

"Come on, you Marines."

It hurts to have to walk out into that hell of dread—the open beach without cover and with Suribachi towering on the left, the airfield ahead grim with its guns, the cliffs on the right. They run forward, stooping slightly, and grab the stretcher. The man on it has a belly wound. They carry him to the aid station, where the wounded lie on their stretchers in rows, silent, shivering, trying to master their dread of another hit now when they are helpless. . . .

Seven men crouch ten feet from the water's edge. Under the beached ambrak behind them lies a crushed Marine, and next to him a crushed Japanese. A runner comes slithering through the black sand, with the word:

"Move up!"

Three of the men get up silently and follow him into the open. Two of the remaining four, members of another outfit, look at one another, then at the other two who remain with them, huddled in the shellhole. They realize these other two are dead.

A wave of boats hits the beach and a mortar thumps into the water beside one of the boats, hurling all the men to the deck. They struggle up, cursing and crying.

"Get that thing open. Come on!"

The hinged door of the LCVP swings down and they run out wildly, panting, fall into the black sand, seek shellholes.

Dusk is coming.

Mangled trunks and heads and limbs of Japanese, caught by a shell at their shore defense positions, form a barricade behind which crouch Marines.

Night comes, and the mortars and naval guns hidden on Suribachi and on Motoyama airfield, and on the high rugged terrain to the north begin to howl and cry over-head. They seek the beach they overlook, which is hideously lighted by Japanese starshells and flares.

"This takes twenty years away from my life," said one Marine.

THE CHARGE THAT FAILED was the slug I typed above the next story. It was probably composed late D plus 1, based on a talk with one of the men, and numbered out of sequence.

IWO JIMA, VOLCANO ISLANDS, BONIN GROUP—(Delayed)—Even Marines retreat.

Iwo Jima is barren and open, and the ground rises cruelly from the beaches to Motoyama airfield—for whose possession many young Americans have already died.

Across the black sand, sinking to the ankles with each step, and torn by ruthless Japanese artillery, mortars, and small arms fire, charged a unit of a famous Marine regiment—one of the most gallant and tragic charges of the war. It was this morning—D day.

Like the Light Brigade at Balaclava, or Pickett's Virginians at Gettysburg, a pitiful few reached the prized airstrip, and dug in, and then could not hold their ground. Shaken and exhausted, the remnants fell back through fresh waves of advancing Marines. They were being reorganized late in the afternoon, as this flamethrower unit, part of the command of Major Charles C. Berkeley, Jr., of Vista, Calif., pushed past them up from the beach to aid in what will be the decisive assault on the airfield.

"About 200 of us made the charge," said one of the survivors, PFC (check rank) Roy Cline, 22, of Lenoyr, Tenn. "I guess a few of us made it. They began to spray us with mortars. We couldn't take any more, we had to go back."

Tonight the airfield is still at least partly theirs. Tomorrow it will be wholly ours.

The next dispatch of which I have a copy was done after the shock of the landing had passed. I was trying to summarize the first phase of the battle, following the landing, as I knew it. The Pickett-like charge is there; Poe is invoked, of course; and the dying man on the beach—with the corpsmen beside him with "uptilted bottle"—is undoubtedly the man whose soul I had encouraged to depart in my poem. This is the only dispatch in which I briefly stepped outside my total focus on the 4th Division's area to pass on what men said about the taking of Suribachi, a mile to the south.

The slug at the top of the page, left, is MACABRE BATTLE.

IWO JIMA, FEBRUARY 24—(Delayed)—This battle has been a weird and ghastly story by Edgar Allan Poe.

It has been an artillery duel—without the depth and width of front which lessen the terrors of artillery. The men have only so many square yards within which to deploy and dig in, and then the artillery lashes them. We have not been able to destroy the Japanese artillery quickly, as we did on Saipan.

On the most violent beaches—the Blue and Yellow beaches—D day's dead are still unburied. Mainly they are our dead, for there was little hand to hand fighting. The guns and rockets of our ships, tanks and land-based artillery have killed many, but most of their dead were buried by the Japanese behind their lines. All around us are ours.

It is cool by day and cold by night. Sometimes clear and sometimes rainy and dismal. The uniforms are bizarre. We wear dungaree coats, under them brown woolen shirts, and over them Marine field jackets or Seabee rain jackets. We lie at night huddled in dead men's blankets, carry dead men's weapons, drink water out of dead men's canteens.

It has been a macabre fight in a trap. The trap was formed by crossing artillery and mortar fire from the strange volcanic dome of Suribachi on the left, the high ground beyond the airfield in the center, and the cave-studded bluffs on the right.

We entered the trap by our own choice, because the only beaches were there. The Japs zeroed in on each wave of landing craft, and the men who survived dashed through the surf and up the heavy black-sanded slope for the first of the terraces—to fight on up to the great redoubt which is the airfield, Motoyama. By the fourth day, the left jaw of the trap—Suribachi—had been severed from the enemy.

Suribachi was taken with the support of fire so intense that men swear the contour of the volcano was changed. Giant flakes of rock were ripped from its sides as the honeycomb of caves and their guns and men were burned out of Suribachi's sides.

Heroism was one with terror. Men did not have time or dare to realize the chances they took.

Three sailors were taking three shot-up Marines out in a landing craft to a hospital LST. The boat was struck by mortar about 30 yards out. Each of the sailors grabbed a Marine, and swam back to shore with them. They begged another landing craft to run the gauntlet of mortar fire and the perilous surf, and took the Marines out safely.

A gunnery sergeant, in charge of a shore party group carrying ammo from the beach, was nearby when a small dump caught fire. A larger ammo dump close by was in danger. He leaped into a caterpillar tractor—which he had never driven—and began to scoop the blazing material down into the water. The "cat" and the gunnery sergeant caught fire, and he was carried out of the blaze by his buddies, critically burnt.

A company of Marines made a Pickett-like charge up 500 yards of open ground. They suffered grim casualties—clutched a corner of the all-important airstrip—but lacked strong enough tank support to hold it in the face of fire and secure it.

On the beaches the wounded lay fearful, shivering and begging to know if the beach had been "catching it." Their greatest dread was another hit. The breath of life barely stirred within one man. His face and body were already the color of death, but the plasma kept pumping in frantically as the little Navy corpsman stood beside him with the uptilted bottle. Finally the veins refused to take the plasma. The tube was inserted into the penis. The breath of life flickered, the struggle with the elements was visible. The man shuddered and rolled his head, and there was a moment of hope, and then the earth-hued stillness blanketed him and sadly the little corpsman drew the poncho over him, rolled it back a moment as an afterthought to check the dogtag number, then drew it over his face again.

At night, the weird battle became an eerie carnival, with the brilliant green and red and blue lights of our ack-ack rising majestically over our helmets to form a great Christmas tree of defense. A Japanese bomber droned fearfully through the steel boughs of this tree, to drop its eggs three hundred yards away near the beach where our buddies were dug in beside ammo dumps and heavy gear.

Then the mortars whistled like ghouls just overhead. Our foxholes shook when they landed.

Of all my dispatches, the one that got the widest play was written on D plus 5 or 6 when I went to the beach once again. Suribachi had been taken by the 3d Division, while for ours—the 4th—the battle had moved away from the beach to the high ground north of the captured airfield. The Japanese artillery had been taken out, and their mortars could no longer reach the beaches.

It seemed to me bitterly ironic that the story that had the least to do with the frenzy and terror and exhilaration and horror of combat should be the one that got the biggest dis-

tribution, sent out by the News Enterprise Association (NEA).
But even then I must have realized that it was a part—and
a vital part—of the total texture of the great battle, and must
be honored. Besides, it was good news, good for home morale.

IWO JIMA—(Delayed)—In less than a week after D-day
on Iwo Jima, orderliness and efficiency replaced the mad
confusion and terror of flying shells, wrecked landing craft,
and equipment jammed hopelessly on the beaches waiting for Jap artillery to destroy it.

Supplies are being unloaded regularly. The bloodsoaked
sand has been flattened into temporary smoothness. Per-
forated steel mats form footing for vehicles to bring ammunition and food to the troops fighting on the higher ground.
Shore parties are organized and staunchly dug in. The
wreckage has been cleared away, and most of the dead
have been buried.

A former Boston lawyer and an Annapolis graduate who
plans to be a watchmaker, both Marine Corps officers,
teamed up as the chief agents in transforming the dread
"Yellow" and "Blue" beaches into supply routes that are
sealing our victory on Iwo Jima.

The lawyer is Lt. Col. Richard G. Ruby, 30, commanding officer of the 4th Pioneer Battalion and in charge of all
shore party work on the beaches assaulted by the 4th
Marine Division. A graduate of Dartmouth College and
Harvard Law School, he is a veteran of the amphibious
victories on Saipan and Tinian. The Annapolis man is his
executive officer, Maj. John H. Partridge, 28, whose wife
lives in Annapolis.

Many others aided in the work. A Marine pioneer captain landed with the assault waves to plan the organiza-
tion of the supply system from ship to shore. He was critically wounded. Seabees landed on D day and hung on to
that beach under the heaviest shelling any American fight-

ing men have had to take during the war. Navy hospital
corpsmen brought the wounded to the beaches and evacuated them to ships waiting offshore—using the same
landing craft that brought supplies from ship to shore. Of
32 corpsmen with the Marine unit on the beach, 14 were
killed or wounded in the first two days.

Now the beach is orderly and organized. Supplies are
coming in. There are strong, well-spaced foxholes. There
is a new look in the eyes of the men on the beach. The
worst is over. Now American machinery is moving in—
the seal of a successful amphibious assault.

In part, that story may have been my try at making it up
to the pioneers. I was supposed to be their combat correspondent but had deserted them to go in earlier with the
assault platoon. I was glad I had, but their captain had a right
to be angry.

As to victory—yes, it had been sealed when I typed that
piece sitting on a stool in the PR tent, but most of the dying
still lay ahead. The amphibious assault, with its torrents of
blood, had been made, the foothold secured, and the first airfield taken; but the high-velocity gun and knee mortar, fired
from dug-in positions and the mouths of caves by men committed to death, meant that every yard had its price. How
dear this grinding and tearing payment was to be I did not
realize.

I cadged a ride to the hospital ship. There one of the combat correspondents, Johnny Barberio, from Mamaroneck in
New York State, lay dying. His leg had been blown off in the
landing, he had gangrened, and they could not save him.

The formal reason for my going was to deliver some dispatches, as different correspondents and photographers took
turns doing. It meant a decent meal and a night's sleep in a
bunk, too.

This stay on the hospital ship was as phantasmagoric as anything that had taken place, as macabre in its way as the macabre battle I had reported. The whole ship seemed a vast white theater of suffering, bathed in painfully brilliant light and splotched with red. Those being saved and those who could not be, those waiting for the surgeon and those undergoing surgery, those being wheeled in and those being taken below, seemed everywhere.

I was desperate to be of some use, and must have helped briefly. But I knew I didn't belong there.

It was a troubled night's sleep on that hospital ship. And in the morning I felt an overpowering urgency to return to the island as soon as I could and share what the others were undergoing. In my novel I ascribed this urgency to my fictional hero.

Back on the island by the first craft that left, I trudged up at once, through the rolls of barbed wire and the ammo crates and the parked tanks and amtracs, toward the lines. The assault platoon was in reserve that day, which meant it was perhaps two hundred yards from the fighting.

Krywicki told me at once that Bill Tolarovich had been killed by a mortar and was already buried. Moriarty had also been killed. On the transport Moriarty had stubbornly predicted his own death, and I had urged him not to be fatalistic.

Eight young replacements, out of eleven who had arrived only yesterday, had been killed that night by an unlucky mortar hit into the big foxhole they had all dug together.

But they had not had time for—anything! It was so unjust.

That night I slept beside Frank Krywicki and two of the other "old" men, in their square foxhole. As the mortars howled we would tense together, then as they thudded somewhere else we would together untense. I felt I belonged there.

The sense of injustice and guilt worked inside me. I had landed and moved up with the assault platoon because I did

not want to land with the pioneer battalion after everything
was secure; but on D-day night the Japanese artillery had
concentrated on the beach, to cut the infantry's supplies and
reinforcements, and the pioneers took losses much heavier
than ours. And it had gone on that way, it seemed to me,
during the next days.

I would leave one outfit and go to another, to get more stories; and the outfit I had left would get hit hard. If I had been
with the assault platoon when the replacements came, I
would have been interviewing them that night when the
mortar round hit. But I had gone off the island, to safety, and
I wasn't even there to grieve over Bill Tolarovich, or the corpsman Joe Genola.

The sense that I was taking up earth-space that belonged
to better, braver, less lucky men, that I had given only a frightened, reluctant minimum and had been unaccountably and
undeservedly spared, would grow like a subterranean echo.
It became an allegory in prose. What I had done and felt
became elements of that allegory. And the image of angels—
this time of one angel flying over that dread battlefield—
returned in force as its vehicle.

I slugged it THE FEARFUL MARINE.

It was growing late on D day, and the fearful Marine lay
curled in a shell hole with some others.

A corpsman came running to them and peered into the
shell hole and begged, "Can two of you give us a lift, please,
down to the beach with a wounded boy? There's only two
of us and he's heavy."

Pride goaded the fearful Marine. It was even stronger
than his fear. He looked at another beside him and said,
"Let's do it," and the other in turn was moved by pride.
They rose and crept through the ringing volleys of shell
and mortar and picked up the wounded man, so that there
was a man at each of the four ends of the bloodsoaked

stretcher, and carried him down the desperate slope to the field aid station on the sand.

And the Angel of Death, in his passage about that terrible island, observed the deed.

And a second time the fearful Marine lay crouched in a shell hole. His buddies had been torn to rags about him. He was terrified and overcome by the horrors through which he had gone and trembled to think of being in the lines a minute longer.

A Marine came back through the lines, holding up a shocked buddy, who sobbed and shook. "Can somebody help me get him back?" the Marine asked.

A second time the fearful Marine volunteered. In his heart he knew he was goaded by his fright, and willing to walk upright through the flying shrapnel rather than endure his terror a moment longer in his hole.

And the Angel of Death was passing, and smiled mysteriously.

And a third time the fearful Marine had a chance to get off the beach for a day, to carry a message to a ship standing by. And he was ashamed—because many of his buddies had been killed on the beach, and others were fighting and being killed at that very time. And he was safe and clean aboard the ship.

And goaded by his shame he went down to the sick bay of the ship, where the wounded were being repaired or were dying, and asked if he could help, and he carried a torn Marine on a stretcher from operating table to sack, and held his head, and held up the plasma bottle so that the plasma ran into the man struggling to live.

And the next morning he ran from his shame and returned to his company on the beach.

And the Angel of Death passed by on mortar-shod feet, and smiled his twisted smile—as if in triumph over a sadly inept opponent.

And the Angel of Death said:

"See, these small good deeds of this Marine were the result of pride, of fear, and of shame."

Then the Angel paused, and added, reluctantly, "Perhaps there was some slight compassion, too."

And the Angel of Death passed by the fearful Marine as he slept, and the Marine awoke the next morning. But many better men did not awake.

The tale of the Angel of Death and the fearful Marine would stay scribbled in my notebook.

*No matter what they do to
stop us, no matter how many
we lose. . . .*

The fallen, the fallen!

7–Chronicle of Blood

They say it takes the very young to fling themselves forward,
to die in battle, because they do not really know yet what
life is about and therefore cannot imagine how different from
life death is. As we get older we become more aware and
therefore more cowardly, or at least less bold. In general, I
would say from my own experience this is true.

Often I reflected that the Marine Corps knew what it was
doing, concentrating on eighteen-, nineteen-, and twenty-
year-olds. How ready they were to do what was asked, and
sometimes more. How careless of their existence.

Ten years older than most of them, I found that under
artillery or mortar fire or bombing, my legs and my whole
body were full of lead from fright. Whenever I had to walk

upright away from the front, helping carry a wounded man, I had to refuse to let my mind work, or I would have been unnerved by fear of a bullet in my spine.

The Japanese bravery in that island war, in the face of overwhelming firepower, is still mysterious and even awesome to me. I could not have endured it. I doubt that our young Marine infantry could have endured it. But maybe they could; there were wells of endurance built into the line infantryman's esprit.

When I clamored to go ashore earlier on D-day, I had no concept of the experiences ahead. There was a refusal to think, or recognize facts—such as the fact that we were nearing Japan itself, and that this penultimate island was crucial to both sides; or to recall my sudden bad thrill when I saw the story about Tarawa; or to imagine what it had been like for the waves that went in on D-day on Saipan and Tinian.

Refusal to think, and failure of imagination—that saving grace.

From beginning to end, it was emotion and will. The power to reason—the desire to reason—was frozen into a dream state. Only afterward, long afterward, it would be possible to look at the war thoughtfully.

I asked to interview prisoners. After a week of combat, there were exactly nine in the 4th Division stockade. Most of the Japanese, from army and navy units alike, who were not killed in battle killed themselves.

I could understand their actions intellectually but not emotionally. It also seemed strange, and unfair, that a people whose soldiers would kill themselves rather than be prisoners of war should lose to a people whose soldiers definitely would not do that. The story of Ario, whom I interviewed, did not solve this riddle but helped me put it into some perspective.

IWO JIMA—(Delayed)—The killing was still going on at the front. The crack "Imperial Marines"—troops of the Special Naval Landing Force—were fighting savagely, and almost to the last man.

Ario was one of the few Imperial Marines to be taken alive. Maybe through him, I thought, it would be possible to get a glimpse into the fanatic and ruthless psychology of those men who died like rats and killed themselves rather than surrender.

Through the medium of our own Sergeant Ben Kawahara, of 145 S. School Street, Honolulu, T.H., it was possible to talk with Ario, as he sat in the prisoners' stockade.

Ario turned out to be a handsome, broad-shouldered, stocky lad, with honest, soft eyes, slow and earnest speech, and a shy expression.

He had been brought up in a rural district on the main island of Honshu. As a boy, Ario said, he loved to walk to a hill overlooking the nearest small harbor, and watch the ships as they came in from the blue sea, and sailed out again toward the horizon.

Ario did not want to go to war. He changed from one high school to another (which specialized in vocational subjects) in the hope of escaping the draft. But he was not much use on the farm, after he finished his school year.

His parents believed firmly that East is East and West is West, and that Japan's sphere was the East and the Western nations should not meddle. They told Ario he might as well enlist in the army, and help win a part of China, so that the Japanese people might have enough room and so that the East should be happier and more united.

"That is the way I was taught," Ario explained.

On Iwo, he was assigned the duties of a suicide anti-tank man. He was to run out of a cave and hurl grenades under the treads of our tanks.

After a few such missions, Ario was too terrified to run out any more. He crouched in his cave, with another Imperial Marine, and they hurled grenades out at the advancing Americans. The time had come to die.

But Ario discovered that he wanted very much to live. He was only 18. If only he could have one or two more years of life!

The officers and schools had drilled into him the conviction that the Americans would torture him and kill him anyway. But he wasn't sure. And he didn't want to take his own life. He heard the interpreter calling on him to give up. He cried out that he was willing to surrender.

In the stockade, he is amazed that he is treated with kindness, fed, and clothed. He is so grateful, he says, that he is even willing to fight in the American armed forces in return for this kindness.

As to his future, Ario is blank. To his parents, he is dead. An urn with his supposed ashes and with his photo in it has been sent to them. If he ever returned to Japan, he and they would be shamed—he would be "the one who surrendered." If he were told to return to Japan, he would have to kill himself. Of that he is sure. But life is sweet, and he enjoys watching the American ships in the harbor and the great American planes soaring over him.

Watching Ario, and hearing his words reconstructed by Sergeant Kawahara, we could not help thinking of the old proverb: As the twig is bent, so will the tree grow.

After that first week, I resumed a kind of beat that lasted through the rest of that month on Iwo.

There were the lines, where I could crouch in terror and talk with the men, taking notes, and sometimes share one of the assault platoon's foxholes; we would shudder in unison, coiled against one another, as the mortar thumped near us.

There was the beach, where I could pick up tales in the evacuation tent or from the pioneers, or sit watching overlooked corpses of Marines bob face-down in the water, and meditate—without thinking. And there was going back, a bit sheepish and guilty, to the huge PR foxhole to decipher my notes, collect my ideas, and type up my stories.

But once it was as terrifying, for me, in that huge PR foxhole as anywhere on the island. The Japanese managed a night bombing.

No outsider can in the least understand how it feels to lie helpless, tensed so that your anus seems to be up in your neck, hearing the bomb shriek down, and how the whole system clogs with terror when it strikes. That was as bad, for that brief hour, as the mortars.

Within a few days, however, the last of those Japanese bombers had been taken out.

Sitting outside the tent the PR captain finally rigged up, I submitted to be photographed by Gene Jones; he set it on a timer, so the two of us were photographed together. Gene's twin brother, Charley—the future sportscaster—stuck a bottle of saki into the sand at my feet, lending an ambiguous touch to that portrait of a grizzled, unshaven old Marine with the young one during a battle-pause. The two brothers took some of the finest combat stills done on Iwo. Gene was now carrying a Thompson submachine gun.

I would wander back and forth between those poles of my beat—the lines, the beach, the PR foxhole, crisscrossing the debris of battle and its fearsome nearness, and the weirdly incongruous sulphur mounds special to Iwo, visiting the areas where men were moving up on the line and areas to which units that had just been replaced on the line had moved those few yards into reserve, and men bivouacked on the beach, and men foxholed beside their tanks, and men on guard over ammo dumps, and being evacuated in ducks from the beach. In the course of all that wandering, one picked up stories that floated there, already oral history but evanescent as bubbles that would disappear and be lost, and the deeds and the anguish lost with them in a little while . . . except for the few who would always keep them locked inside.

And sometimes, as in the case of this tale of the modest hero I got from pioneers on the beach, no one would have had much to remember, there being no name attached. Or the story of the three Marine buddies—which was really a collage but absolutely true, because you could multiply Joe and Bill and Johnny many times.

IWO JIMA—(Delayed)—This is the story of the Anonymous and Modest Hero.

It might also be called The Haunted Ship of Blue Beach.

Every night terrible mortar and shell and rocket fire raked the troops and ammunition dumps on the beach.

It was uncanny. The Japanese held no high vantage points from which they could spot our dumps and concentrations. But the hits were being scored, and men were being killed.

Far behind the lines, gutted, and beached in the black sand, leaned an old Japanese transport. It was a grisly evidence of the American bombing and shelling before D day.

The Anonymous and Modest Marine was either patrolling or asleep on the beach.

He waited for the next mortar burst, and watched the stars, and glanced at the old gutted Japanese junk.

Something ghostly stirred in the bomb-burned hulk. He listened. He heard a low, steady sound.

Either a droning voice or a constant tapping.

He leaned over and stirred another Marine. They got a couple more. They crept up on the dark derelict as it sprawled at the water's edge.

They made a rush, and there was a scuffle, and shots.

There, in the empty black hull, lay a Japanese artillery observer, a radio sending set strapped to his back.

From his hiding place in the ship he had been observing the Marine dumps and concentrations and guiding the deadly Japanese artillery fire.

This is the story as it comes through the commanding officer of an infantry battalion, and other men who don't spread false stories.

But although everybody on the beach has heard the story, nobody knows who the Marine was who saved so many lives and so much valuable ammo. Either he had no buddies nearby to blow his horn, or he "got knocked off" soon thereafter, or he is just modest.

Therefore this is called the story of the Anonymous and Modest Hero.

IWO JIMA—(Delayed)—The blood of Lura T. Matheyer, given at Oakland, California, on St. Valentine's Day, February 14, poured into the collapsing veins of a shattered Marine on the beach at Iwo Jima, 12 days later.

The blood of Frank McKee, donated on the same day at the same center, stood ready in a pint bottle—packed in ice in a wooden box with a spun glass lining—waiting for the next desperately wounded Marine who would be carried down from Hill 382 or Hell's Acres.

For the first time the Marines on the beach were getting whole blood, given by American civilians. Several hundred pints, donated on the West Coast and flown to Iwo Jima, have already been given by Navy doctors and corpsmen to the most badly wounded.

Usually a unit of whole blood is given together with a unit of plasma. Whereas the plasma combats shock and gives the wounded body the raw materials to build up new blood, the whole blood replaces directly the blood which the wounded man has lost.

The whole blood is taken from donors whose blood is the universal, or "Type O." Each pint bottle carries a tag giving the name of the donor and the place of donation.

IWO JIMA—(Delayed)—There were three Marine buddies—Joe, Bill, and Johnny.

There are three airfields on Iwo Jima.

They landed under mortar fire and advanced through the black sand up the steep slope toward the first airfield. Halfway up, a direct mortar hit killed Joe.

(The next day the airfield was won, and soon the bulldozers were at work, and the Seabees were hauling dirt up the slope for grading.)

At the lip of the second airfield, in the unforgettable and desolate ground known as the Wilderness, an anti-tank gun fired point blank, killing Bill.

(Soon the second airfield was secured, and work was in progress, and Hellcats and Mustangs were landing on the first airfield and taking off again to drive the Japanese from the rest of Iwo Jima.)

Beyond the Amphitheatre, near the third airfield, a rocket bomb flew at midnight. Among those who slept in that foxhole and never awakened was Johnny.

(Do you hear the roar of the motors, the angry whirr of propellers? The fighters and bombers are taking off from the airfields for the Japanese mainland, destroying the factories and war weapons of the fascist military clique—striking from only 650 miles away, like a short left hook to the heart of a reeling boxer.)

And that is the reason why Joe, Bill and John have died—with 4,000 others.

They were infantry, but now they fly on every mission with the angry roaring of our planes.

Marines, and infantrymen everywhere—in our war, in Korea, in Vietnam—created resonating names for the battle places: "Heartbreak Hill," "Hamburger Hill" (a favorite, with its image of the grinder of human meat), "Death Valley," "Flame-tree Hill," "Hell's Acres," "Turkey Knob," "Charlie-dog Ridge." "Suribachi," of course, was imaginative enough. Sometimes the height designations on the maps did the work of the imagination: "Hill 382." But usually the men preferred to bestow their own monickers, which became part of the intimate history of those who had been there and survived.

The same process worked in me. I assigned emblematic names to places and areas in that dreadful wonderland that was the 24th regiment's territory of about one or one and a half square miles.

There was the bowl-shaped depressed stretch in front of the ridges that had to be taken for the battle to be won. I called it—following others—the Amphitheatre.

There were the sulphur mines, with their poisonously gleaming, greenish yellow mounds. They became for me—conjuring up Poe, Dürer's woodprints of Hell, and my own romantic dread and excited wonder—the Brimstone Pit.

And the entire blasted, shattered, Dürer landscape over which the division's three regiments advanced, in little rushes, in cringing pressed to earth, in attacks on cave by cave, on fixed-gun bunker by bunker, in thirty or forty deaths a day—I called the Wilderness.

I probably had in mind Grant's punishing victory in the Civil War. But for me the name became a central, darkly poetic part of my personal history; and I needed to tell the world.

IWO JIMA (SULPHUR ISLAND)—(Delayed)—In the Wilderness, where the second battalion of the 24th Marine regiment spent four days on the line, there is no quarter and no respite from the song of death.

The song is sung by mortars, among the desolate crevices and gouged shellholes of the Wilderness. An accompaniment is played by rifles and machine guns, keeping the men down in the crevices and shellholes where the mortars can get them.

The Wilderness covers about a square mile inland from Blue beach 2, on the approaches to Motoyama airfield no. 2. Here the fighting is so ruthless that men must steel themselves for every movement, to rise to their knees, to jump from one shellhole to another, to creep forward, to creep back.

There is no cover. Here and there stands a blasted dwarf tree. Here and there a stubby rock ledge. Among the maze of volcanic crevices and shellholes, the eyes of converging bunkers are slits in the sand. The bunkers cover one another, and the mortars cover the approaches to each series of bunkers.

The second battalion attacked with flamethrowers, demolition charges, 37-millimeter guns, riflemen. A tank advanced in support, but was knocked out by a mortar. After every Japanese mortar volley, Corsairs streamed down on the mortar positions, ripping their charges of rockets into the Wilderness. But after every dive was ended, the mortars started their ghastly song again.

Cracks in the earth run along the open fields to the left of the Wilderness, and hot smoke seeps up through the cracks.

Gains counted in terms of 100 or 200 yards for a day, in terms of three or four bunkers knocked out. Losses in terms of three or four men suddenly turned to bloody rags after the howl of an unfortunately lucky mortar, in terms of a flamethrower man hit by a grenade as he poured his flame into a bunker.

The assault platoon of flamethrowers and demolition-
ists, spearheading the regiment's push through the Wilderness, lost two assistant squad leaders killed. A third had
cracked up beneath the mortar fire on D day, but returned
to carry on through the Wilderness.

A veteran flamethrower-bangalore combination carried
a bunker which had been a Japanese observation post.
The assault platoon moved its headquarters in under the
steel and concrete roof. The Japanese raised a mortar bar-
rage, scoring direct hits on the roof of the bunker but being
unable to destroy it.

The platoon's sergeant—Sergeant Frank Krywicki, of
Grand Rapids, Mich.—bounded out of a shellhole as the
mortars ranged in. Out of the sand emerged two heads—
Japanese occupants of a bunker unobserved until then.
He whipped up his shotgun and splattered the heads.

"Am I glad I packed those two extra shotgun rounds
instead of the iodine bottle I wanted to take," the sergeant
mused afterwards.

The platoon's lieutenant crouched behind a rock as a
heavy mortar howled over and exploded fifteen yards away.
When he raised his head, he saw a severed finger lying
beside him. He looked at his own hands, then examined
the hands of the two men crouched beside him. All were
intact. The finger belonged to one of three men in the hole
fifteen yards away, whom the mortar had struck and torn
into three bloody rags.

The commanding officer of one of the infantry companies and an assault platoon sergeant got two other men,
grabbed a 37-millimeter gun and hauled it around the side
of a shellhole to range in on a bunker. They drew direct
gun and mortar fire. They swung the gun around, and ran
it around to the other side of the shellhole. From there the
officer fired point blank to destroy the occupants of the
bunker.

Another commanding officer insisted on leading his men out into the Wilderness again in spite of a wound in his penis. A private—PFC Jean-Marie Bellemere of Auburn, Me.—became furious when his squad was pinned down by mortars and machine guns while a buddy lay helplessly wounded and needing evacuation, so he grabbed a flamethrower without orders and charged a pillbox and poured flame into it, consuming the Japanese inside. Then he ran through the sniper fire to find a poncho, and he and another man carried their buddy out of the Wilderness.

Toward evening the Japanese mortar fire was so heavy that the battalion had to pull back, giving up about fifty hard-won yards, ground paid for in blood.

They left two flamethrowers, to be regained by the morning offensive, and carried their wounded back to first aid stations.

When the battalion moved out of the lines the next morning, the men who had been four days in the Wilderness felt as if they had lived 40 years.

I had managed to make myself follow my prime hero, platoon sergeant Frank Krywicki, into that Wilderness. Mortars started to hit behind us, and I tumbled into a hole. There I found a scrap of letter and was so fascinated and then moved that I almost forgot to be afraid.

When Frank bounded ahead again and called back to me, I stuffed those rumpled pages into my dungaree pocket and ran after him. Later, I copied the letter. It became a dispatch I never sent.

THE LETTER

IWO JIMA—(Delayed)—The sulphur shells were bursting in Hell's Acres, just north of the awful airport, and east of the Brimstone Pit.

(A letter lay abandoned in the bottom of a rocky foxhole.)

All morning corpsmen had been walking through Hell's Acres, finding the dead.

("Dearest Darling, How are you today OK I hope. The baby is fine and hope you are the same. Honey I didn't get any mail as yet this week. I hope I get some soon. Honey I don't know what is wrong but I guess it is cause you are on the move. Honey I know you will write as soon as you can. Honey I didn't get any mail since the 26 of Jan, I hope I get some soon . . .")

The remnants of a company of the 4th Marine Division were awaiting the word to move up again. They watched the corpsmen carry away the dead and crouched low when the sulphur shells hit ninety feet away.

("Honey I love you dear and hope you are still in love with me as I miss you very much and I do love you very much too. Honey please write to me as soon as you can Honey. Please Honey I don't know what is wrong . . .")

The fighting in Hell's Acres had been terrible yesterday, and in the morning, and now there was only the desolation of acrid earth, and ripped rocks, and torn barren trees, and the gleaming weird green-yellow mound of sulphur which marked the Brimstone Pit.

("Honey the baby is getting along in school he likes it very much he gets a star in all his work . . . Please write soon Honey . . . Honey he said to me today that he wishes his daddy was home to help him with his homework too. Well Honey . . .")

The last page of the letter is lost.

The morning's and yesterday's dead had been covered with ponchos and carried down the crags from Hell's Acres for burial. The living now moved up, toward where the sulphur shells fell and the mortar howled and the sniper's rifle snarled. Toward the Brimstone Pit and the last terrible mile to the sea.

A sight about which no dispatch was sent: the "meat wagon," a truck heaped high above its sides with the bodies of our dead. The bodies at the top bounced lightly, as if on gentle springs, as the truck nosed carefully over the uneven terrain.

Our dispatches avoided such raw and close-range scenes. This was not due merely to censorship. We accepted the war as a just war, so our restraint came from within. We had to report truth, but total battlefield truth could injure morale. That was understood by civilians as well, and we had to understand it even better.

The meat wagon scene would go into my novel, five years later.

Once I went into the Marines I left the question of our war's transcendent meaning to others. Let them make the overriding ideal statements, so that these heroes' deeds (and mine) would be placed within a moral universe. I was all done with that, and could quietly and anonymously go on with the business of falling, one among many, rifle pointed ahead, shielding the simple rose of freedom with my heart.

Still, sitting on a ridge of black sand at the edge of the area marked off for the 5th Division cemetery, I knew that the slight young chaplain was speaking from those heights I had abandoned; and I was vaguely thrilled. (Later his speech was mimeographed and passed around, and I stashed a copy.)

His words barely floated to me, and my attention moved in and out. I was composing a dispatch in my head, and paragraphs of my story and of his speech must have shuttled in and out, like alternating presses:

"This is the grimmest, and surely the holiest, task we have faced since D day. Here before us lie the bodies of comrades and friends. Men who until yesterday or last week laughed with us, joked with us, trained with us. Men

who were on the same ships with us, and went over the side with us as we prepared to hit the beaches of this island. Men who fought with us and feared with us."

This highest rise in this bleak ground—without doubt the core of the fierce Japanese resistance on Iwo Jima—was won and lost and won and lost and finally won again.

Several battalions took part in the winning and losing, and lost men and officers, and were fed replacements, and lost more men and officers, until finally they held the high ground but were chewed up and exhausted and faced a mutilated but still vicious foe.

"Some of us have buried our closest friends here. We saw those men killed before our very eyes. Any one of us might have died in their places. Indeed, some of us are alive and breathing at this very moment because the men who lie here beneath us had the courage and strength to give their lives for ours."

The men who won the high ground for the first time, losing many of their buddies, knew that the ground would be lost again, and won again.

"We just softened it up for the next guys," said PFC Nyles Schmidt, of Phoenix, Arizona. "And it needed a lot more softening. At night we had to withdraw—they were throwing in mortars—and they crept up again and took some of their positions back. But not all of them."

"All that we can ever hope to do is follow their example. To show the same selfless courage in peace that they did in war. To swear that by the grace of God and the stubborn strength and power of human will, their sons and ours shall never suffer these pains again. These men have done their job well. They have paid the ghastly price of freedom. If that freedom be once again lost, as it was after the last war, the unforgivable blame will be ours, not theirs."

"One of the anti-tank guns hit us," recalled Sergeant Eugene E. McCurry, of Duncan, Oklahoma. "It hit the antimine boards on our side and blew them off. It jolted us up, that's all. Another tank ahead of us was knocked out completely. Then we got this gun. After that we were working alone on that ridge."

"Here lie men who loved America because their ancestors generations ago helped in her founding, and other men who loved her with equal passion because they themselves or their fathers escaped from oppression to her blessed shores. . . . Here no man prefers another because of his faith or despises him because of his color. Here there are no quotas of how many men from each group are admitted or allowed. Among these men there is no discrimination, no prejudices, no hatred. Theirs is the highest and purest democracy."

A company commander—one of the most famous in one of the greatest Marine regiments—walked through the foxholes toward the desolate ridge. His company now held one sector of the Thrice-Won Ground, some 1500 yards from the sea. He was a man who was dead-tired and so accustomed to death that he walked toward it now with the mien of a man walking to work. He slouched, with a springy padding step. He was thin and young.

"We tried to move five times, today," he said over his shoulder to a sergeant who looked up inquiringly from a foxhole. "Every time we lost men and we couldn't move. Going to try again now."

He shrugged his shoulders as a man would over a tire that had gone flat and needed fixing, and nodded his head in a friendly goodbye, and padded forward.

"And any among us the living who fail to understand that will thereby betray those who lie here dead. Whoever of us lifts his hand in hate against a brother, or thinks himself superior to those who happen to be in the minority, makes of this ceremony and of the bloody sacrifice it commemorates an empty, hollow mockery."

Fox and Easy, as well as George, had lost over half their original strength. Many of the men were replacements. Few officers were left. One company had just lost its fifth commanding officer.

"When the last shot has been fired, there will still be those whose eyes are turned backward, not forward, who still will be satisfied with those wide extremes of poverty and wealth in which the seeds of another war can breed. We promise you, our departed comrades: This too we will not permit."

A stray dog out of the Japanese lines had grown friendly with the attacking Marines. They fed it, and the mongrel followed a squad of demolition men as they advanced on a cave. The men had no idea where the next bunker was, and they advanced quietly. The dog barked. Reluctantly one of the men turned and drilled it with his M-1.

"We come first," he said.

"Thus do we memorialize those who, having ceased living with us, now live within us. Thus do we consecrate ourselves, the living, to carry on the struggle they began."

The sixth effort by George company gained 25 yards. One cave had been knocked out, and a little path hacked forward through the corner of Hell. The troops dug in.

"Too much blood has gone into this soil for us to let it lie barren. Too much pain and heartache have fertilized the earth on which we stand. We here solemnly swear: This shall not be in vain!"

All night the Japanese mortars hammered into the face of the high ground. The stretcher jeeps could be heard running up to the ridge and stopping and starting again after they were loaded. In the morning the attack began again.

Over this Thrice-Won Ground—the key to the defense of Iwo Jima—the 4th Marine Division fought forward yard by yard and death by death.

"Out of this, from the suffering and sorrow of those who mourn, there will come—we promise—the birth of a new freedom for the sons of men everywhere. Amen."

Even through my growing bitterness over the carnage, which by now had overwhelmed my confidence in glorious outcomes, I had to recognize the sincerity of the young chaplain's words.

The last days of Iwo are a blurred montage of experiences, whose chronology is hard and painful to reconstruct:

Using a chunk of the platoon's C-2 explosive to heat coffee, and setting fire to myself. When I finished rolling in the sand, my face was burned and eyebrows singed off. One of the "old men"—the ones left of those who landed on D-day—shouted joyfully, "You can get a Purple Heart! You can get a Purple Heart!" And I shouted back frantically, "No! I don't rate one!" And I didn't, of course.

Again in shamed fascination, watching the graves registration men heave bodies onto the meat wagon till they were piled like carcasses of steers.

Sitting in the sand beside little Webb. He was the "damn good little man, good on the Marshalls, Saipan, Tinian," who had cracked up during the landing. He got hold of his nerves and made it back to the platoon, and I had just sent a long dispatch about the reckless heroics of "The Man Who Came Back." Now he was being evacuated with a stomach wound, and I was trying to reassure him.

Going up with a squad from the platoon on a cave-blowing detail, carrying one of the satchel charges—I still can see, and feel, myself treading carefully in the steps of the man ahead of me—and cautiously setting it down when Frenchy was ready to take it up to the cave's mouth. . . .

My heroic platoon sergeant, Frank Krywicki, was wounded toward the end of the battle. What was left of the assault pla-

toon was attacking the remaining bunkers using flamethrowers, bangalores, and satchel charges. There was a labor short-
age: most of the old men had been killed or wounded, and
most of the replacements had been wiped out on their first
night in their king-size hole by that direct mortar hit.

Krywicki began to go up himself to the mouth of each
bunker to cover the flamethrower or demo man. He could
not stand the thought of any of his men being killed when
he was not there. ("How would I feel if that happened?") His
knee had been twisted and he twisted it again every time
he scrambled ahead or back; but as I lay crouched in terror
in a shellhole, he bounded out of it and bounded ahead like
a goat to point out a position to the demo men. He shepherded the remaining raw men, warning them to keep their
eyes on the ground for mines and making them disperse as
they were supposed to.

On one of those very last days he went up with one of the
demo men to take out a bunker that had been giving them
trouble. The demo man hurled in a satchel charge, but the
man inside must have crept almost to the mouth of the cave
to grab the charge and hurl it back.

It exploded against the demo man and blew him into frag-
ments. Krywicki, five feet away, was spun around twice and
knocked flat. All the buttons had been blown off his shirt,
and he was deafened. (One ear would never regain much
hearing.) The demo man's scalp, with all the hair still on it,
flopped like a mop beside him. Krywicki told me, "I thought
sure I was dead."

He got up and staggered away. But the bunker still had to
be taken out. He called his one remaining squad leader, Donald Breier ("a twenty-two-year-old from West Toledo, Ohio,
who had never played high school football and who was
always trying to find out how the Toledo High football team
had made out," I carefully recorded). They went up together
with a satchel charge, blew up the bunker, and sealed it.

By now the platoon was down to seven men. All the rest
were marked KIA or W&E or MIA in Krywicki's rollbook. Only
four of the men who had made the landing were upright. Krywicki could not hear and kept getting dizzy spells. The lieutenant, LoPrete, ordered him to go down to the beach and be
evacuated, but he refused. "There wasn't hardly anybody
left," Frank later explained to me, by way of apology. He always
spoke of himself apologetically, querulously. He kept going
up until the last bunker was sealed, on the last day.

Dear Kitty,
Tomorrow we should secure. I do not believe I will go to
the front anymore, for I am exhausted and up to my throat
with death and fright in all their forms, and I only want to
go away and meditate about it. So I am writing you, and
will send the letter away tomorrow, right after we secure.

I am okay. The days and nights behind stretch like some
half-understood nightmare of emotions and thoughts and
sights and experiences. I want to have a chance to grieve,
for you cannot let yourself go here. Bill Tolarovich, of whom
I wrote in my last letter, was killed by a mortar. Joe Genola,
the corpsman I liked so well, was killed too. Of the platoon
I went in with, most of them are dead or wounded. I can
find no reason that I should have come through, except as
an admonition and a mortal responsibility. Do you remember the correspondent who welcomed me at the Marine
barracks, telling me, "Now Dan, the thing to do here is to
relax." Bill Vessey. He was killed. One of our fellows was
killed. Another from the other division, photographers too.

I ran the gamut of ways to be terrified—at least I do not
want more. Kitty, as we came in on D day, a mortar hit
beside the Higgins boat, knocking us all down, and then
the boat hit the beach, and it was hours later that I realized the explosion had blown my glasses off my face. And
at the other end of the spectrum is the time I was finish-

ing taking a leak when a sniper sighted in on me and had
me grovelling in urine and excrement while his bullets
cut the sand beside me and I couldn't help giggling.

It is a desecration to laugh or even to live normally, but
the horrible thing is we do. And nobody would have stopped
a minute over me. The whole process of humanity seems
frightful and nauseous. I will refuse to forget our dead in
the shellholes and the trucks and awaiting their graves—
and their smell will pursue me always. Toward what hate-
ful far-off event can all this drift? Why are the sweet and
innocent taken? Who am I to persist? There is something
wrong, something terribly wrong and askew and awry. I
will write more as soon as I can. When this letter comes,
you will know that I was all right when we secured. (I
burned my face with gasoline cooking chow, but it is now
healing; I don't think there'll be any scars.)

Goodby, Kitty . . . I do not want to go through this again.

Dania

Four thousand Marines were reported dead. (The final toll
would be nearly 7,000.) At the island's far end, the Japanese
commander had performed ritual suicide, joining his 23,000
men in death. The great battle had been decided.

THE FIFTEENTH OF MARCH was the slug I put on the last story
sent from Iwo.

In the hall of heroes, reserve a place for Marines who
fell on the front lines while the graves of their comrades
were being consecrated a little way behind.

On March 15, the day after Iwo was announced "secured,"
the 4th Marine Division dedicated its cemetery.

The day was bright and cool. The wind whipped the
flag in the square known on the terrain map as "165 Love."

Hands were raised to helmets in the final salute to comrades, then "thrown away" as the bugle's threnody ended.

Meanwhile, on the line George company faced the last pocket of Japanese, containing them against any infiltration, cleaning them out so that the remnants could not mass for a suicide charge.

A twenty-year-old sergeant, Jesse Murphree of Lyon, Miss., had been wounded twice in the battle. Each time he had returned to George company. He led one of the platoons.

"There was a man," said a George company rifleman.

"If anyone in his platoon was hit," said another, "he went out to get him, no matter how much hell was flying around."

"An inspiring leader and a vicious fighter from the day of landing until his death," wrote the battalion commander afterward.

And so it was. One of Murphree's men was hit. Murphree ran to the man's side, and was struck by a shell fragment. He stood upright and called for a corpsman, then was struck again and went down.

One of those who answered his call was Cliff Guse, of Milwaukee; he was killed on the way.

In 165 Love, the men had gathered in three groups. The Protestants stood or sat bareheaded in the sand. The Jews stood with helmets on, before a youthful chaplain who wore a black skullcap. The Catholics knelt bareheaded, before their chaplain in the vestures of his faith.

The wind which whipped the flag bore out to sea the mingled sounds of their litanies, and singing:

"Rock of Ages—"

"*Yisgadal v'yiskadash—*" arose the age-old Hebrew kaddish—prayer for the dead.

"Hail Mary, full of grace—" a responsive murmur from the men kneeling on one knee, arm flung over the raised knee and bare head lowered.

Behind rose the cliffs, and there George company was still fighting.

Another nineteen-year-old Marine, PFC Donald Bartholomew, from Lancaster, Pa., carved with his combat knife on a sandstone rock the name of his wife, Kathryn, his baby's name, and his own name. He went back to bring up chow, then started up again toward his foxhole. A sniper shot him through the neck, and he died instantly beside the rock with the names cut into it.

Three others who fell there on the 15th of March were Private Edward Waczak of St. Paul, a twenty-seven-year-old BAR-man who had cornered thirty of the enemy in a pillbox and had directed flamethrowers who burned them out; twenty-four-year-old Sergeant Arnold Cork of Midson, Ill., a onetime Western Union messenger boy in Granite City, Ill.; and twenty-six-year-old Private Jerry Laluch, of Flint, Mich.

The prayers were over, and Marines walked up and down the rows of crosses, as if walking through a sad garden in which these crosses grew in orderly profusion, with here and there a Star of David blooming.

Later that day the six from George company were brought down from the cliffs, and joined with their buddies. Graves 1722, 1730, 1742, 1747, 1754, 1761. . . . The graves that separated these men who had fallen together contained other Marines, for George company had not been alone on the lines.

This was how the cemetery was consecrated. . . .

As I wandered the beach in the hours before loading, my mingled sense of dedicated grieving, exhaustion, and relief was complicated further by a brief meeting.

I came across a black Marine—the first I'd ever seen—sitting on the beach. He scowled back at me.

In 1941 the Marine Corps had finally started drafting black Americans. None had been assigned to combat, but on Iwo—this I read only later—four all-black "labor companies" under

a white commanding officer unloaded ammunition and supplies onto the beach and were cited for coolness under fire.
This youth was either one of them or a replacement brought
in to patrol the island along with Army troops. But there was
no enemy to patrol against; all had been killed or had killed
themselves, except the few like Ario who surrendered.

He looked angry. If he felt cheated of the glory of having
been "a combat Marine," serving instead as a stevedore, I
could understand. At the time I briefly felt bad for him, and
because my sense of a sad triumph was jarred.

I said something foolish, like "It's a rough little island." He
just said, "Aw, shit," and looked aside in anger and disgust.

I was sure he had wanted as much as I had to fling himself forward on freedom's altar—with as much sense of what
that phrase might mean, from his vantage point, as I had
from mine. I hesitated, wanting to say, "You'll get your chance."
But it would have rung false.

And I couldn't care enough. I'd gotten mine.

Our loading for the return from Iwo Jima was a time of
complex emotions—pride and humility, exhaustion and anger,
vast relief and guilt because of it, and an aching regret.

I loaded early and settled down on the deck. Sitting there,
I was swept by an overwhelming sense of the connection of
myself and all the others who had survived to those who had
fallen, and an overwhelming need to express a vast common
grief on behalf of all of us. I began to write in my notebook:

WE CLASP OUR FALLEN

We clasp proudly and fiercely to our breast
Each single one of the fallen
The fallen in the sea, on the beach, storming
  Suribachi, charging the airfield, taking
  each cave, each pillbox, each bunker

The fallen carrying the wounded and giving
   them aid under fire
The fallen carrying messages
The fallen on patrols
The fallen by mortar, by rocket, by high-
   velocity gun, by machine gun, by
   rifle, by land mine, by anti-tank
   gun, by grenade

The fixers of chow
The diggers of "heads"
The luggers of ammo
The keepers of records
The firers of BAR, M-1, carbine, machine gun
   light and heavy, of mortar, the drivers
   of tanks and of halftracks

The fallen composed, and the fallen twisted,
   resting as if in sleep, on all fours
   curiously squatted, under the poncho
   sprawled with careless hand flung over
   face, or under the poncho with guts hanging
The fallen recognizable and unrecognizable
With and without dogtags, to be given burial
   as known and unknown
The fallen without words, the fallen who
   whimpered, who shrieked,
Who were given blood in hope, and without hope,
   through arm, leg, thigh, buttock, penis
Who spoke to the priest in a last whisper
   and whom no priest was near
Who knew and did not know, who feared and
   did not have time to fear, who cursed,
   who sobbed, who prayed, who begged to
   be killed quickly

The sweet boys like flowers in the sun—
    knowing fun, food, whiskey, cloudy climbing
    and star-swinging
The sweet boys who were sure of one thing
    —that they would return
The wearers of medallions to avert any
    evil, the loved of religious mothers
The worshippers of fathers, the correspondents
    with hometown girls
The lovers, and the boasters, and the too young
    and shy to have been either lovers or boasters
    (the fallen often deflowered and the fallen
    still virgins)
The junior ends, senior tackles, flashy
    passers, substitute running backs
On the little teams in the numberless elm-
    bordered high schools in the numberless sad
    towns bisected by lonely night-hooting
    railroads

The fallen, the fallen!
The buddies, the sharers of foxholes,
    the tellers of stories, the dreamers
    without words, the singers without music
Our fallen, our fallen!
We clasp them—once and for good—
    mightily, tearfully, each to our breast.

I scribbled all of this seated against the rail of the transport as it lay off the island, slowly filling up with the living and the spirits of the dead.

I see the Odyssey of those who were of the epic
That one day will be sung
That one day will be sung when the world
* is colder and the stars have shifted*
That one day will be sung in pity and wonder
* and harshness and grandeur*

8– The Long Road Back

The return voyage from Iwo:

The men lay on their sacks or on deck. They stirred as little as possible. At night the ship was blacked out. During the hot days, however, the Navy crew pulled away the hatch covers and the wind came down into the troop hatches.

The junior officers played bridge. They too moved around infrequently. They did not inspect the men, or enforce regulations. The staff officers noted this with some disapproval but they knew they could not ask officers who had fought, eaten, defecated, slept, and grieved together with their men to change back quickly to the other way.

The junior officers, and even the staff officers, said nothing if a Marine came up on the upper deck to sleep in the shade, or to read. They would have been ashamed to send him down. But very few men took advantage of such latitude. They did not care now. They did not want any favors. They were filled with one curious feeling, while empty of almost all else—a bitter, cynical, hard pride in themselves. They carried with them what they had undergone, what they had endured, what they had survived. They carried with them all the dead. In this bitter pride they were self-sufficient, and scorned gratitude from any but themselves.

Some nights I lay on my back, as I had before, looking up at those pitiless constellations. I knew an important part of my life was finished but was not ready for a new part to begin. This state of mind would continue much longer than I would have believed possible. No uplifting vision of freedom's altar, or freedom's rose, interrupted it. I had done what I had set out to do but was no longer sure what that was. I suspected there were complications I had not foreseen in the world's nature. That poem in which I had called on the star to "fall, shrieking and burning, from high happy ceaseless perfection" would have been appropriate now, if I had not already written it.

I also caught myself watching the other men of our regiment as they leaned on the rail, as they spoke to each other, as they stood in the chowlines, as they just sat or lay silent, thinking or reading. And what struck me, suddenly, was that these were not kids but mature men. They had experienced, survived, and matured.

Most of them had come out of high school into the Marines and then been thrown in death's way over and over. They had needed no college. Danger and death and everything that went with these things had made them grow up. Whatever I had gained by being more fortunate in formal education, they had gained by another route—and more surely.

I was astonished at how clear this insight was. I had not set it up or expected it. I knew it was important and should lead to further understanding, but it also raised a galling question: was taking part in the things we had done and seen the only way for most young men to gain an education and maturity?

My new sardonic feeling was increased by the scene at the dock on Maui. As the Marines trooped down from the ship, they were met by a welcoming committee. The Red Cross workers and the wives and daughters of local sugar and pineapple growers were grateful and sincere—I know that now, looking back. But the contrast between these well-dressed, mainland-bred women and the men in their battle dungarees, still saturated with their experiences of fright and death, was stark. Leis were hung around the men's necks, and doughnuts were handed to them. The leis ran out after a while—I noted in my anger—but there were enough doughnuts for each man to get one.

I described in my novel the wrenching irony and pathos of that scene—the men, still carrying inside them their dead, each receiving a doughnut.

> He would never forget. If he forgot it would be to his endless shame,

I have my character Lewicki insist to himself.

And in me it must have been about then that the confusion began to take shape, over whether I had really come back or been left Out There, on the Pacific islands with the other dead.

Back on Maui in our sea of tents, amid the hot aimlessness and the aimless liberties, the pristine beaches and luxuriant nature, the curving mountain slopes, the Hawaiian rainbows, I wrote up commendations for medals: Purple Hearts, Bronze Stars, Silver Stars, Navy Crosses. One of the Silver Stars was for Krywicki. I also wrote letters of consolation.

Dear Mrs. Z——:

I only wish I could tell you more about your husband, and the circumstances of his death. I knew him very slightly, and thought of him always as a straightforward and attractive man, full of life and good humor. I have talked to others about him, and have heard the men whom he led in battle reminisce about him. Without exception, they respected him, and his death shocked them as the death of no other officer they lost. When I talked to his superior officer, the colonel of the battalion, I noted the tenderness and sorrow in his voice as he said, "You know, Charlie died."

One of the men who had served with Captain Z—— since before the division left the state, Sergeant Major John M. Gale of Leonia, N.J., who is still in the pioneer battalion, said: "I will always remember him as a real 'Good Joe,' just as I remember my father."

You already know the main circumstances of his fatal injury. A sergeant, James W. Conway, applied a tourniquet to your husband's leg, and then he and another man carried Captain Z—— to the aid station on the beach. They tried to reassure him that his wounds were not bad, but he said, "Don't kid me." Men who made the trip by Higgins boat to the hospital ship with him say he was calm and self-possessed, an example to the other seriously wounded.

I realize there is no real consolation for such a loss. If anything happened to me in battle, I know the only con-

solation for my wife would be that it was part of the great
price we were all paying for a future world in which our
two-year-old boy can grow up without fear or danger.
Most sincerely,
S/Sgt Dan Levin

The men were given questionnaires to fill out so that Joe
Blow stories could be sent to their hometowns. They were
asked especially what kind of information was desired by
the home folks.

One man who had been through Tarawa, Saipan, and Iwo
and had had one furlough in that time, wrote that the home
folks did not want the truth.

> The glamorous side is all they want to hear, the real
> part of war isn't believed or [is] listened to with a bored
> feeling, such as: the constant waiting, baking in the sun
> all day the flies all day & the mosquitoes all nite, the hr.
> on & hr. off all nite, the rain & shivering all nite, the thirst
> & the same canned ration all the time till it becomes taste-
> less paste that you spit out, the always incomplete "word"
> never being told what the situation is. Further more an
> admission of fear is either regarded as weakness or mod-
> esty in a combat veteran. They don't realize that without
> fear there can be no courage.

He ended with his definition of combat, which struck me
with its stripped-down—and cynical—realism: "My own
opinion of combat is [that] it is nothing more than life boiled
down eliminating the inbetween pauses. The death & injury
& sickness are found all thru life so why the hell get excited."

The terrible battle for Okinawa was still on, with its fixed
positions, heavy infantry losses, and its special horror of
kamikaze planes smashing into our ships.

Germany's surrender hardly stirred a ripple on our faraway
Maui. Our fates were enclosed by the Pacific.

European victory had made clear that the war would end in victory. But it still had to be ended, by somebody. More Army troops would now be transferred to our theater. But the Marine Corps was already preparing to assault the southernmost island of Japan itself, Kyushu.

I was transferred to an air wing based on Oahu. The theory, which seemed reasonable, was that a combat correspondent could be trained to double as a tailgunner.

But there was no élan—in me, who had been stripped of my precious identity as a combat correspondent of the foot Marines, or in the men around me. The would-be tailgunners and the others in that hut waited heavily in their bunks.

The scuttlebutt was that one hundred thousand wooden boxes had been shipped to Oahu, looking toward estimated KIAs. And that might be only a down payment. Kyushu was a big island; Honshu was even bigger, and we who had come from the infantry knew this enemy. The suicide plane strikes off Okinawa had only confirmed our suspicions about what still lay ahead. The atmosphere was something like that during the mop-up days on Iwo: we knew that some would have to die finishing the job.

Then suddenly something happened that changed everything. I did not write down my reactions and those of others until later, but I have tried to recall them precisely because that is important: it might be of use in the debate today over how we really feel about our stupendous atomic technology.

At first I did not quite believe—did not want to believe—the headlines about an atomic bomb destroying Hiroshima. It must be another heavy bombing, maybe heavier than most.

I read the story, and then several of us talked.

"Sounds like a lot of poor fucking Jap civilians got it," someone said. "Must have been worse than the San Francisco quake."

"You can say that again."

"A fucking holocaust," the first man said. He stared at the paper. "This ought to do it."

There was no joy in this news, nor in the news that followed about Nagasaki, even though some of us may well have been saved from death by those strikes. Our boxes were ready.

I have tried to be precise about how I felt, and how I'm sure others did. I think we felt foiled, tricked, betrayed, cheated in some vital way, as if all of us had lost some of our essential manhood and importance. Things had been lifted out of our hands into the realm of the powerful, inhuman laws of mechanical nature.

I can swear there was as much dread as relief. We were grateful for being reprieved, but we were not glad at all.

The news of the Russian attack in Manchuria came. The war was ending. We heard the text of the Japanese emperor's proclamation on the radio. It was over. Everybody who could get anything to drink drank that night. Somebody got hold of firecrackers, and they burst over Catlin half the night. The merriment was half-hearted, and half-puzzled. It's over, we kept saying to each other and to ourselves. It's over. We knew there ought to be joy and struggled to evoke it.

On this strange, ambiguous, and chilling note the greatest and most awful adventure of my times was concluded. Everything for which all that warm young blood had been poured out, everything so doggedly chronicled in my dispatches, all the grieving and all the sacrifices, had been ended abruptly by a humanly harnessed but superhuman, human-diminishing power.

I was left with confusion and doubt and dismay about the future. All the quandaries were about to return, all unsolved.

But anyway, I was returning.

Returning proved more roundabout than I expected. On the way back from North China in December, I lay on a bunk in a transient barracks on Guam, awaiting my papers. Near

me I heard a Marine talking, and suddenly I got goosebumps.
I grabbed for my notebook to get his words down.

I did not even see the man. He was either lying or sitting
on a bunk two down from me; the barracks was mostly empty.
He talked to his buddy, delivering a monologue in a proudly
disdainful, proudly complaining drawl—a Marine beating
his gums. But I recognized a classic statement of the poetry
of the Marines.

"You get the shitty end of the deal. You bury your dead
and send the wounded to the hospitals and those of you that
are still alive go someplace else and get knocked off your-
selves while the Army comes in and gets the glory. . . . But
that's the Marines. There's the kind of outfit it is. You asked
for it, didn't you, so don't look for no pity. You'll get trouble
wherever you go, that's what you're here for."

That voice rang a chord in me, and in the unseen speaker
I recognized myself. This mock-heroic pliant entwined with
pride in a prodigal throwing away of the self—of course it
lay at the bottom of the psychology of those who became
Marines. And so it must lie in my psychology as well. We
had both asked for it.

Maybe he had said, directly and powerfully, what I had
furbished and prettied up with "freedom's altar." Was there
really anything besides duty and fear and the pride of being,
like him, one of them?

We stood against the rail yearning toward the shore,
toward the lights of San Diego, toward the world we had
left once, in a past age, and which was, we understood
somehow, shattered and swept away, without being
bombed, invaded, destroyed, but more subtly, in ourselves
and in those we had left, a metamorphosis.

In my green uniform, with my bars and my discharge
emblem and my division patch and my battle ribbon with

the stars on it, I rode on the train and the train moved toward Washington.

Awhoo-o-o-o-ooooh, it cried, and the wheels under me pounded, and a plume of black smoke trailed backward, black smoke trailing back, back, back, to the West Coast and beyond, over the wake-winding sea to the desolate isles. . . .

Awhoo-O-O-O-OOOOOO . . .

Coming back, coming back, come back, coming back.

Do you hear me? I don't want to come back. I am lost, somewhere out there. I was killed on D-day, February the nineteenth. No, in the Wilderness. No, I was killed on a bluff near Garapan, on the slope of Mount Tapotchau, near Tinian Town. I lie with arms spread, and the red poinciana flowers fall on my face, and a huge rock snail has made a home in each of my eyes. . . .

Awhooo-ooo-ooo-ooo!

Coming back coming back coming back coming back.

Awhooo-OOO-OOO-OOOOOOO!

In the dining car a well-built young woman asked if she might sit at the table and I said of course she could. She sat across from me, and we ordered food and also drinks. She told me she liked my looks, and I told her I liked hers—and I did. I knew there was a problem, but I was not sure what it was.

She told me she would not mind stopping in Washington with me, and going on from there.

"I always pay my own way," she assured me.

I nodded. That sounded reasonable.

I think I insisted on paying for the food, but we split the drinks.

The train was pulling into Union Station, and she got up and I got up and we went down the aisle. She climbed down first, and I took a step after her and, bewildered, looked down into the eyes of my loyal wife waiting for me on the platform.

"Home Is the Hero" is probably a fair reflection of my inner
state during the next months.

> I remember
>   Olziewski and Lane and Delwig
>   and I remember
>   me
> I remember
>   the terrible sun with its
>   nightmare sinking
>   and the green moon of death
>   and the stars without pity
>   and rainbows around the rest camp
>   and loading again and sailing again
>   through seas enchanted
>   your whole life's vision mounting
>   until the searing morning
>   climbing down the nets. . . .
> this I remember
>   as I walk the pavement
>   this I remember
>   as I drink my whiskey
>   I take a drink for Olziewski
>   and I take a shot for Delwig
>   and I take a slug for Lane
>   and I take three slugs for me
>   and now if I can get home
>   I'll flop on the bed.

I was helped, lovingly and patiently, by my wife. Others
helped. But finally I had to help myself. Circumstances in
Washington made finding a way of getting myself together
more urgent.

I had returned to a New Deal–type agency whose corpse
was being ingested by the State Department. Men who once
had clout now had no role to play, no reports to write for pres-

idents or for Congress, no one needing to consult them; they
sat or wandered morosely in silent offices, cleaned their fin-
gernails, or talked in tired, hurt voices about things of which
they were no longer a part. They were as much ghosts as
my dead Marines piping on Saipan island.

For my part, I sat in my cubicle typing furiously the start of
my war novel. I was saving myself by staying Out There, eight
hours every day, oblivious to the catastrophes around me.

A notice to report to the State Department forced me to
interrupt my work. I walked, reluctantly, past the Lincoln
Memorial and into the old building on Pennsylvania Avenue.
I climbed to the second floor, then couldn't find the handle
on the door and kept trying to push it open. Finally I got it
right and walked in to confront two young men in pinstripe
suits and bow ties—the uniform of that most traditional of
departments.

"There was no fucking way I could open the fucking door,"
I said. They regarded me with startled apprehension.

Then I returned to that island of the nearly dead on Con-
necticut Avenue and resumed hard work on my novel.

In the pause between chapters I looked out on the traffic,
or sat dreaming—evoking the sun-shot deck, and on it the
bodies of men dirty and browned and naked to the waist in
their sweat-black dungaree pants, moving about restlessly,
waiting in the ship-girdling chow lines, sleeping, horsing
around, playing poker or pinochle, thinking morosely. (How
morosely Moriarty brooded, reading his future by some Celtic
insight.)

> I see my buddies, become immortal,
> Drifting on that transport, not to battle
>   and anguished death, but toward an enchanted
>   and happy island, on a sunshot sea,

umbering into nocturnal, wizard-purple
distance . . .

By the time the novel was completed, I had weathered the
transition and was able to move in the stream of postwar
American life.

The roots of liberty are fed
  by streams mysterious and unsung;
Potomac dogwood trees will bloom
  From seeds by Saipan's flame-trees flung.

9-The War God's Legacy

Years passed. Wherever I was and whatever I was—State Department reporter at the UN, Paris expatriate on the GI Bill, Ohio businessman, college teacher—I kept believing in myself as a writer, and I kept remembering with pride that I had been in the Second World War as a Marine.

But I also kept suspecting I had left the real me Out There, on some Pacific island. The fantasy worked quietly, internally.

This split between outer life and inner fantasy was sharpened by the pressures and stresses of a new age, with its amnesia. The brave deeds I had sung seemed irrelevant to what a later generation cared about or believed. The movie

"The Best Years of Our Lives" pictured well the hurtful and ruthless relegation of those brave deeds to a private past. And soon Vietnam threw its corroding shadow over the remaining memory of "the righteous war." Meanwhile, as if in protest, the image of the war years in which I had lived so keenly, endured and risked and felt comradeship, only grew and threatened to make them more real than the present ones.

That was when the theme for a poem came to me—first in a dream, which meant it came from deep inside: a dream of a Marine forced by an inner power to seek for something, half-knowing and dreading what he may find.

Sitting in my office in the humanities building on a Long Island campus in the midst of preparing for a composition class, I suddenly started to type the poem instead. I forgot where I was and only came to, reluctantly, when the poem was finished. The students had long since dispersed.

In my poem, a veteran of World War II "in devious wandering, by forsaken paths" comes on the scene of an old firefight—rusted machine guns, gear, and M-1s strewn about, shelter-halves. With a sense of purpose he follows a downward slope to the edge of a stream, where he comes on the remains of a Marine, the skull face down. When he turns the form over,

> The face was there, all undecayed; and having
> found what he had wandered all the world to
> prove could not be found, and feared the most
> to find, he stood there in the ravine beside the
> desolate village, in the impenetrable forest,
> waiting for the coming burst of tropic rain.

I knew this poem had to do with the universal longing for youth, but also that it had to do especially with my fantasy; and I knew that the way to deal with a fantasy was to expose it.

I put the poem away.

For a long time, the idea of facing those islands again—
in real life, now, not in dreams or poems about them—must
have been too daunting. But whenever things got tough I
could always think of returning and finishing my life Out
There.

Another decade passed before I was ready.

I headed for Saipan. Iwo I could not face yet. That could
come later.

On Continental no. 644, Tokyo–Saipan

Again those intolerable, aching, into-eternity-reaching
clouds. One becomes part of this nature without resistance or effort. Yes, if defeated by life this Pacific might
make the most sense. But even if there is not a complete
defeat, but only to respond to the romantic quality that
has always been mine. I cannot, simply cannot, finish my
days on Long Island.

On one level, I must have expected to find it all still there
in frozen action. All that image needed was one breath of
reality to crumple into dust. I must always have known that.

But in such cases, as in love, it is never any use to be prepared. Finding prose where there had been the burning tears
of poetry—those ghostly Marines circling and piping under
that flame-tree, around the musing oriental girl—was a shock.
But worse than having to face the knowledge that the poem
had died was having to face a living new reality: a Saipan
that had nothing to do with me, the Marine combat correspondent of my war.

Prose it was. An interesting though still isolated island of
13,000 souls, at first glance very American, a tiny new com-
monwealth with problems and ambitions like other segments

of the United States. Trying to decide about being linked to
Guam, wanting to retain some independence, too many people living on food stamps, pollution threatening. . . . There it
was: a Chamorro kind of Long Island.

With—what I had not expected—a Japanese dimension.

Digesting the reality I still did not believe, I sat on a stool
at the Trader Bar in the lobby of the Continental Hotel—one
of a string of opulent hotels, chintzy-lush. Its lobby opens at
both ends into brilliant sun, brilliant flowers, and palms.
Beyond, the kidney-shaped swimming pool; then the white
beach and vast Pacific sea and sky. (Those were the only
things I recognized; they had stayed—reassuring, consoling
constants.)

In the lobby, honeymooning Japanese couples and Japanese tourist groups sauntered or sprawled in wicker chairs.
I had to grin wryly. They were reconquering Saipan, by simply being near enough and willing, even eager, to come here.
Behind me a gift shop, like the gift shop in any American
second-string hotel, was loaded with tourist goodies.

I took some bearings. It was probably a few hundred feet
from here that I had sat desperately typing on another summer day: "This is an island of the dead. The dead are everywhere. They lie in their strained postures of death. . . ."

It had no meaning. There was no relation.

I was early for my lunch interview with the island's leading
entrepreneur. I finished my drink and walked down sandy paths
lined with cowries and snail shells, bordered by hibiscus,
bougainvillea, plumeria, banana and flame-trees, coconut
palms. There was a shuffleboard court and a volleyball court,
both splendidly landscaped. Next door, the French airline's
hotel was equally gorgeous. Bathing beauties, mostly from
Japan, lounged beside the pool, and on beach chairs facing
the ocean. There were thatched-roof shacks to change in; most
of the bathers padded from and to the hotel in their bikinis.

At the beach's edge, camouflaged by wild grass growing atop it, was a pillbox. There was a gaping hole through it—must have been hit by a shell from one of our five-inch naval guns. I stood in front of it for a few minutes. It was as out of place in that lush, lolling atmosphere as my whole vision of Saipan was.

Joeten arrived, shaking hands all around on his way toward me—the way my business acquaintances in Cleveland always did. We started for the fancy hotel restaurant, with its smorgasbord of Chamorro, Japanese, Carolinian, and Western foods. What I would remember of that lunch and interview was having to thread our way, going there and back, through throngs of Buddhist priests from Japan, with shaved heads and swinging robes. They had come to pray for the souls of the thirty thousand Japanese who had died in the battle for Saipan, and to commit their bones to cremating flames.

Government-organized excursions had been coming for years, I was later told. The men wandered hillsides and marshes and climbed into caves, finding the bones of their dead and collecting them. After cremation the ashes were taken back to the motherland.

I was terribly touched, and it hurt to know that I had never thought with any real sympathy about those forms strewn over the island after we had mowed down their hopeless attacks. I had begun to feel so much lack of care, in my country. These people cared.

In a rush of piety I thought about going out with the next batch of Japanese bone searchers, but I did not. Instead, I rented a cart and drove around with a map until I found the area where the division cemetery must have been, where the combat photographer I called McLean and the captain had been buried. There was nothing there, of course. The ground was clean. Our three thousand were dug up and shipped back long ago. I should have remembered that. Dwarf trees grew here and there, and the soil seemed good; that was all.

It's good to bring the bodies of those you loved back for home burial. But it means that these faraway islands, where their blood ran out, remain forever far away, even more far away. How can they, I thought, become part of the heart of America? For Japan these places have meaning. Japanese priests find the bones and take the ashes home, but honeymooners come from Tokyo and Kyoto and all the Japanese cities, and Japanese businesses come, and Japanese settlers. So there is a replanting.

Few Americans come. A few old Marines and old soldiers. It's too far, and costs too much. There is almost no remembrance. My haunted island of the dead does not exist. It was conquered by nothingness. The living island that exists is a real but unknown island.

To stave off the nothingness and bind past to present, those who so reverently searched for the bones of the dead Japanese followed a ritual, assembling them and placing them on tangatangan branches and burning them, chanting prayers as they did so. The souls of these dead had to quit the earth after thirty-three years. By now, I supposed, the ceremony only helped in the cases of some tardy ones. But cynicism did not help. Everything these priests were doing hit too close to home. I caught myself yearning to be part of their ritual.

If I had left an important part of my spirit here, as I seemed to have made myself believe, it had by now surely risen with the spirits of all the grim and gibbering and gesticulating and wailing Marines, and the spirits of the Japanese we had bulldozed into mass graves and whom the emissaries of their families had so carefully found; and I had better go about growing a new spirit to replace my departed one.

In this frame of mind I left Saipan and took a Cessna plane, piloted by the female half of an American husband-and-wife team, over to Tinian. This time, I resolved, there was to be no quixotic yearning to relive the past. A sentimental tourist visit—

now that was something else. San José, where I stayed in the
one hotel overnight, was just San José—not my Tinian Town.

In the morning, however, in a rented Datsun, I set out for
the airfield over whose tarmac I had walked with the advancing Marines.

The narrow road was deserted. A single quail whirred out
of the car's path. The road narrowed to a car's width, both
borders overgrown with tangatangan. After a steep down-
grade the paving ended, and there was only a dirt road leading to the top of a rise. There I faced the airfield—deserted,
hidden by overgrowth, isolated, forgotten, lost.

I drove slowly down the runway, which led to a bay, then
drove past to another bay. All was absolute silence, except
for the car's sound. No human being could have come there
for ages, surely; not since the age of the battle now so unreal.

I lost my bearings, turned the wheel, and started driving
slowly at random, till in a bay I spotted a low marker. I got
out of the car and read the inscription, which I later reported
in an op-ed story for the *New York Times*.

NO. 2 BOMB LOADING PIT
ATOMIC BOMB LOADING PIT

The legend that followed, in smaller capitals, read:

From this loading pit the second atomic bomb
ever to be / used in combat was placed aboard a B-
29 aircraft and / dropped on Nagasaki, Japan, August
9, 1945. The bomber was / piloted by Maj. Charles
W. Sweeney, USAAF, of the 509th / composite group,
20th Air Force, United States Army / Air Forces, on
August 10, 1945, at 0300. The Japanese Emperor /
without his cabinet's consent, decided to end the
Pacific war.

Around the corner of tangatangan, in the bay about
100 feet off, I read the other marker.

NO. 1 BOMB LOADING PIT
ATOMIC BOMB LOADING PIT

From this loading pit the first atomic bomb ever to be / used in combat was loaded aboard a B-29 aircraft and / dropped on Hiroshima, Japan, August 6, 1945. The bomber, piloted by Colonel / Paul W. Tibbets, Jr. USAAF, of the 509th composite group, Twentieth Air Force, United States / Army Air Forces, was loaded later in the afternoon of / August 5, 1945, and at 0245 the following morning took / off on its mission. Captain William S. Parsons USN was / aboard as weaponeer.

The markers stand there in the stillness, on the forgotten airfield; behind each, its plumeria and its coconut palm.

I turn the Datsun around, and by pure luck find the path I came in on. I drive back seven miles that seem 70, of absolute emptiness. I try to understand.

It's as if nobody wants or dares to have the world know this place; yet nobody wants, or dares, to efface it. There is no agreement about these atomic strikes, only strong emotions. Those who made the decision about the bomb loading pits had to temporize: to mark the sites, but not well; to preserve them, but barely, for—a hundred years? a thousand?—until history and humanity can reach a verdict. . . .

Back in San José, a thoughtful Chamorro woman tells me that the pansy-like flowers before the markers are called chickiricka. "It means the small bird that is always singing around, you know." And "the fruit of those coconut trees never ripens," she says. "It always stays small and long. I think maybe it is still radioactive there."

It was an objective story from the Tinian of our time. It showed I understood that the Tinian of the Marines laid out in rows, of the flares at night, of the flame-trees shedding their flowers over the youth for whom time and space had ended, did not exist. That Tinian may have been an illusion; if not, then prehistory. There was no connection.

Instead I had stumbled on something strange and frightening and of global importance; and I had stood at arm's length and reported it.

Then all at once I saw I had not been all that disconnected from those markers whose messages I had copied so coolly. We were connected not only by that moment on Oahu when I stood stunned, feeling we had all been betrayed by the act that spared so many of us and ended the war. A year earlier, when we walked across that silent Tinian airfield past wrecked Japanese planes, we were assisting in the atom bomb's terrible drama. Without us, those B-29s could not have risen from their bays. We were all involved.

And victory and tragedy, for everyone, were prophetically bound in the innocent song of the lovebirds circling the cliff above Tinian Town that summer evening in 1944. I just didn't know it.

Living and working in Korea, I realized I was still not untangled from the net of that war long past. I had put away, years before, the poem about the man who searches for what he is afraid to find. On Christmas vacation in the States, I started rooting among files, uncovered it, and made it into a story. It would be dramatized for broadcast by BBC radio.

The man in the story has been a ne'er-do-well ever since war service in the Pacific. "He had lost something out there. Or just left it behind him."

Younger men with whom he goes out drinking talk about him.

"This guy ain't all there," one said.

"It's like time stopped on him," said the second.

He pulls himself together enough to visit one of those

islands where he fought. There he goes through the same kind of disillusioning experience I had gone through on Saipan. Finally he rents a car and drives away from town and up the slope of a mountain (Mt. Tapotchau, of course), searching. The road ends, and he gets out of the car and follows a path that descends. . . .

And so he came on the glade in the valley without surprise. A shaft of late sun cut past banyan trees into it.

He arrives—the story following the same script as the poem as if by inner necessity—at the scene of that same firefight . . . walks downhill toward that same purling stream . . . and talks to himself, about their perimeter, their last stand.

He goes on slowly toward the stream's bank, digging his heels into the marshy ground, to where rags that might once have been dungarees outline a form. The last of the day clouds. A squall of warm rain roils the stream.

Standing with both feet in the water, he spots the rusted helmet, picks it up, sees the hole at the temple where the bullet went, and puts it on his head; then stands there, bent, hands on knees, intently looking into the water.

The sun must have rolled out of the cloudbanks as it sank, and a last brightness entered the clearing and illuminated the stream. An image trembled there. He put one hand out and with a finger touched the vague shadowy forehead. He rippled his finger along the stream's surface, tracing the firm, still undecayed, forever youthful face. Then, having found what he had come across the world to find, he knelt down in the stream and stayed that way. The tropic rain came suddenly again, heavy this time, and fell, and fell.

Rerunning the dream, seeing again my double spellbound forever in his doomed glade, should have ended my fantasy. It was high time.

Real things had taken place. The impassioned promises made by that young chaplain over the Iwo graves were being at least partly kept. There was less discrimination, and more civil rights; my country was still flawed, but I had watched it painfully becoming a less cruel and a fairer place. And what we of our war had put out—many so much more than I—had something to do with that. Those spirits ought to be satisfied.

But I soon found that there was at least one kick left in the emotions that powered the fantasy.

Sitting at breakfast on an American military base in Korea, I read in *Stars and Stripes* that Americans could now visit Iwo Jima. A weather station was maintained there. I would have to fly from the American base at Yakota in Japan.

I began to arrange to fly to Japan. It was simple enough, but I arranged and arranged, got a friendly captain to give me a military pass (which I did not need), and took a bus filled with soldiers to our airbase near Seoul, to find that the flight to Tokyo that day was overbooked. That seemed an omen.

I spent the night at a lodging on the airbase, feeling flushed and coughing, and instead of waiting for the next flight took the bus back to Taegu. I returned to my apartment, planning to start again the next day, but became really sick that night. It was the worst fever I'd had in many years. I lay in bed, helpless. When I thought about staggering up and starting for the airfield again, the flu went into my chest.

This struggle went on for a week, until I had to admit I was too terrified to return to Iwo. All the primal fears and dreads that I had played on in the poem about the dead Marines were loosed for real. I had escaped once, I had survived where far better men hadn't; I could not escape twice. As soon as I realized all this, my fever subsided and the flu lifted.

Instead of going to Iwo I began work on a new draft of "Out There." And I was sure I was free of my war, finally. But this was not so.

In the following years I had to accept that what had so worked on my imagination, guiding prose and poetry but also guiding my acts, was all too real and would hold me in a bondage of memory through the rest of my life.

I decided that none of us "who were of the epic" could be freed, or would want to be freed—except in death, and even in death most of us would ask for our bodies or ashes to go into a military cemetery.

A part of me had gone into that poem of the dead Marines and would always pipe along with them for youth destroyed.

But in return for this bondage had come many rewards: The pride—ironic for me who once claimed to believe in an egalitarian world—of having been part of an elite of those more ready than the rest to "lay ourselves down on freedom's altar"; a new identity for the onetime immigrant child and disillusioned young radical, within the American mainstream; the confidence that came from certainty that my offering of myself had taken place in the greatest war ever fought, and the private conviction that the day of February the nineteenth, nineteen hundred and forty-five, D-day of Iwo Jima's month, would be the center of all our age's memories and legends.

The war, and service in the Marine Corps, had been the vast and overriding fate able to rescue me from circumstance and give me an image of myself as actor in a heroic myth, an image we all need. That image still persists, in spite of batterings that challenge me, and all of us—and our country too—to retain pride in self or else go under.

Everything the god of war had promised, he delivered. Morality was not his game, yet even a moral cause he could accept into this one war. At least I so believed, and must defend this difficult belief against time and change, which mock all causes.

About the Author

Born in Russia and brought to the United States by his parents during the civil war that followed the 1917 communist revolution, Dan Levin went through the Great Depression and then joined the Marines, taking part in the battles of Saipan and Tinian as well as Iwo Jima. After service in the State Department as a reporter at the United Nations, he published his widely praised war novel *Mask of Glory*. Of his later books, the best known is one in which he returned to his native land for a subject—*Stormy Petrel*, a biography of Maxim Gorky that places the writer in the context of the Russian revolutionary movement until his death under Stalin.

Levin has owned and managed an insurance agency, been a writer-in-residence and a university teacher, taught creative writing in Korea, worked as a news editor on the English edition of a Korean-American newspaper, and served as a visiting professor at the University of Odessa just as the Soviet Union was collapsing. He still teaches creative writing workshops on the C. W. Post Campus of Long Island University.

The **Naval Institute Press** is the book-publishing arm of the U.S. Naval Institute, a private, nonprofit society for sea service professionals and others who share an interest in naval and maritime affairs. Established in 1873 at the U.S. Naval Academy in Annapolis, Maryland, where its offices remain, today the Naval Institute has more than 100,000 members worldwide.

Members of the Naval Institute receive the influential monthly magazine *Proceedings* and discounts on fine nautical prints and on ship and aircraft photos. They also have access to the transcripts of the Institute's Oral History Program and get discounted admission to any of the Institute-sponsored seminars offered around the country.

The Naval Institute also publishes *Naval History* magazine. This colorful bimonthly is filled with entertaining and thought-provoking articles, first-person reminiscences, and dramatic art and photography. Members receive a discount on *Naval History* subscriptions.

The Naval Institute's book-publishing program, begun in 1898 with basic guides to naval practices, has broadened its scope in recent years to include books of more general interest. Now the Naval Institute Press publishes more than seventy titles each year, ranging from how-to books on boating and navigation to battle histories, biographies, ship and aircraft guides, and novels. Institute members receive discounts on the Press's nearly 400 books in print.

For a free catalog describing Naval Institute Press books currently available, and for further information about subscribing to *Naval History* magazine or about joining the U.S. Naval Institute, please write to:

Membership & Communications Department
U.S. Naval Institute
118 Maryland Avenue
Annapolis, Maryland 21402-5035
Or call, toll-free, (800) 233-USNI.